100 GREATEST
SPORTS CHAMPIONS

Donald Sommerville

SOUTH HUNTINGTON
PUBLIC LIBRARY
2 MELVILLE ROAD
HUNTINGTON STATION, N.Y. 11746

Grolier Educational
SHERMAN TURNPIKE, DANBURY, CONNECTICUT 06816

J 796.
0922
Sommerville

Published 1997
Grolier Educational
Danbury, CT 06816

Published for the school and library market exclusively by Grolier Educational

© Dragon's World Ltd, 1997

Set ISBN 0–7172–7691–0
Volume ISBN 0–7172–7686–4

Library of Congress Cataloging in Publication Data
100 Greatest Sports Champions.
    p. cm.
    Includes index.
    Summary: Examines notable athletes in such sports as baseball, cycling, and tennis.
    ISBN 0-7172-7686-4
    1. Athletes--Biography--Juvenile literature.
2. Athletes--Rating of--Juvenile literature.
[1. Athletes.]
GV697.A1A146   1997
796' .092 2--dc21
    [B]
                               96-50104
                                   CIP
                                    AC

No part of this book may be reproduced or transmitted in any form or by any means, electronic or mechanical, including photocopy, recording, or any information storage and retrieval system, without permission in writing from Grolier Educational, except by a reviewer who may quote brief passages in a review.

All rights reserved.

Editor: Diana Briscoe
Picture Researcher: Richard Philpott
Designer: Mel Raymond
Art Director: John Strange
Editorial Director: Pippa Rubinstein

Printed in Italy

Contents

Introduction 6

BASEBALL
Hank Aaron 8
Roberto Clemente 9
Ty Cobb 10
Joe DiMaggio 11
Lou Gehrig 12
Bob Gibson 13
Willie Mays 14
Hideo Nomo 15
Jackie Robinson 16
Pete Rose 17
"Babe" Ruth 18
Cy Young 19

BASKETBALL
Kareem Abdul-Jabbar 20
Larry Bird 21
Chicago Bulls 22
"Magic" Johnson 23
Michael Jordan 24
Cheryl Miller 25
Hakeem Olajuwon 26
Shaquille O'Neal 27

CYCLING
Jeanne Longo 28
Miguel Indurian 29
Greg LeMond 30
Eddy Merckx 31

FOOTBALL
Jim Brown 32
Dick Butkus 33
Dan Marino 34
Joe Montana 35
Joe Namath 36
Walter Payton 37
Jerry Rice 38
Deion Sanders 39
Emmit Smith 40
Jim Thorpe 41

GOLF
Seve Ballesteros 42

Ben Hogan 43
Bobby Jones 44
Nancy Lopez 45
Jack Nicklaus 46
Greg Norman 47
Arnold Palmer 48
Nick Price 49
Patty Sheehan 50

GYMNASTICS
Nikolai Andrianov 51
Vera Càslàvska 52
Nadia Comaneci 53
Larissa Latynina 54

ICE HOCKEY
Montreal Canadiens 55
Wayne Gretzky 56
Gordie Howe 57
Sven Tumba 58

ICE SKATING
Bonnie Blair 59
Irina Rodnina 60
Torvill & Dean 61

SKIING
Bjørn Dæhlie 62
Annemarie Moser-Pröll 63
Alberto Tomba 64
Matti Nykänen 65

SOCCER
Ajax Amsterdam 66
Roberto Baggio 67
Franz Beckenbauer 68
George Best 69
Bobby Charlton 70
Johan Cruyff 71
Eusébio 72
Inter Milan 73
Gary Lineker 74
Manchester United 75
Diego Maradona 76
Stanley Matthews 77
Pelé 78

Ferenc Puskas 79
Michel Platini 80
Marco van Basten 81

SUMO WRESTLING
Taiho 82
Konishiki 83

SWIMMING
Kornelia Ender 84
Michael Gross 85
Mark Spitz 86

TENNIS
Arthur Ashe 87
Björn Borg 88
Jimmy Connors 89
Margaret Court 90
Steffi Graf 91
Billie Jean King 92
Rod Laver 93
Martina Navratilova 94
Pete Sampras 95

TRIATHLON
Mark Allen 96

TRACK & FIELD
Roger Bannister 97
Abebe Bikila 98
Fanny Blankers-Koen 99
Sergei Bubka 100
Jackie Joyner-Kersee 101
Marita Koch 102
Carl Lewis 103
Noureddine Morceli 104
Paavo Nurmi 105
Jesse Owens 106
Babe Zaharias 107

Puzzle 108
Index 109
Puzzle answers 111

Introduction

Sports come in many different forms and the stories of the champions of sport are as varied, unusual and interesting as the games they play.

This book includes a range of past and present champions from many of the most popular sports played around the world. All have some special quality attached to them. Perhaps they qualify as all-time-greats in their sport because of a long list of world records, or perhaps they are best known for a single outstanding achievement, or for having got where they did against all the odds and by overcoming problems and disadvantages.

Great sporting champions come in all shapes and sizes and nationalities. The smallest and lightest of the champions in this book is probably Nadia Comaneci. Her grace and agility stunned the whole world and not just fans of her sport of gymnastics. What could be more different from that than the power and weight of Taiho, the greatest ever sumo wrestler?

It is easy to see that the basketball players in our book are very tall and that the long-distance runners and cyclists tend to be thin and wiry, but it is far harder to say just what made these very different people into champions.

When you look closely at them all, you find that they do have much in common despite their very different

skills and backgrounds. Jack Nicklaus played golf well almost as soon as he started, but then he practiced hard throughout the time he was growing up. Then he found inside himself the desire to win and the ability to keep playing well under the fierce pressure of top-level competitions. Every one of the champions in this book could tell the same story in a slightly different way.

It is impossible to say whether a champion in one sport is "better" than a champion in another. What we can say is that all the men, women and teams in this book have pleased millions of fans throughout the world and that we can have fun finding out some more about them, too.

Donald Sommerville

Opposite Top Left: Jim Thorpe (football)
Top Right: Bonnie Blair (ice skating)
Below: Joe DiMaggio batting (baseball)

Top: Nikolai Andrianov (gymnastics)
Below: Matti Nykänen (skiing)

Hank Aaron
U.S., born 1934

For many years, one of baseball's most sacred records was the lifetime total of 714 home runs established by the great "Babe" Ruth, but all records are passed eventually. The man who beat "Babe" Ruth's total was Henry "Hammerin' Hank" Aaron with a new mark of 755.

Aaron played for most of his career with the Braves, starting with them in Milwaukee in 1954 and moving with the team to Atlanta in 1966. Aaron's finest moment came in front of his own fans in Atlanta in April 1974 when he hit his 715th home run, off Al Downing of the Los Angeles Dodgers.

Aaron never beat fifty "homers" in a season, but he was always consistent. His lifetime batting average was a very fine .305, and he was also a top-class right fielder. He combined all this with a modest off-the-field personality that brought him a host of fans. However, as one of the first black players to star in baseball, he also met with racial prejudice, especially early on.

Fact File
Professional career: 1954–76
Clubs: Milwaukee (later Atlanta) Braves, Milwaukee Brewers
Career statistics: 3,771 hits, average .305, 755 home runs
2,297 runs batted in

◀ April 8, 1974, and Hank Aaron watches his 715th record-breaking home run sail over the fence. Al Downing of the Dodgers was the unfortunate pitcher.

Roberto Clemente
U.S., 1934-72

Many baseball experts think that Roberto Clemente had the strongest and most accurate throwing arm ever seen in an outfielder. Clemente joined the Pittsburgh Pirates in the National League in 1955. He won twelve Gold Glove awards as the National League's top rightfielder and led the League several times in outfield assists.

He was also a first-class hitter. He won four National League batting titles in 1961 and 1964–66. In 1966 he was also named as the National League's MVP. In his whole career he had exactly 3,000 hits and 1,305 RBI. His lifetime batting average was .317, but he hit better than .350 three times in his career.

▲ Roberto Clemente at bat for the Pittsburgh Pirates during the fifth game of the World Series in October 1971.

Clemente was born in Puerto Rico and had a Hispanic background. He spoke out against discrimination in baseball. Most people now think that he was right to do so and that his talent did not receive the recognition it deserved during his lifetime.

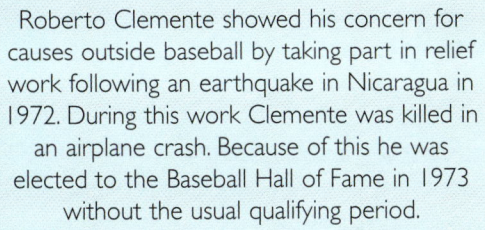

Roberto Clemente showed his concern for causes outside baseball by taking part in relief work following an earthquake in Nicaragua in 1972. During this work Clemente was killed in an airplane crash. Because of this he was elected to the Baseball Hall of Fame in 1973 without the usual qualifying period.

Ty Cobb
U.S., 1886–1961

No one liked Ty Cobb very much as a person. But even though he was mean and unkind, his enemies agreed that he was a great baseball player. He is one of the few baseball stars who earned the right to be considered as possibly the greatest player ever.

Tyrus Raymond Cobb, known as "The Georgia Peach," played as an outfielder for the Detroit Tigers from 1905 through 1926 and then concluded his career with two seasons with the Philadelphia Athletics. He was no great power hitter, but his lifetime batting average of .367 still stands as the highest ever. He topped .400 in three seasons and .300 in 20 more—both records that also remain unbeaten. He won the American League batting title twelve times.

He matched his superb hitting with great work around the bases. He was one of the greatest-ever base stealers. His career total of 892 bases stayed as the major league record for almost fifty years. His great hitting and base running combined to help him score 2,245 runs, the highest career total ever.

Baseball's Hall of Fame was founded in 1935 to celebrate the game's 100th anniversary. The Baseball Writers' Association chooses the members of the Hall of Fame. Ty Cobb's great talents were recognized and he was honored by being the first member ever to be chosen.

▼ Cobb slides into third.

Joe DiMaggio
U.S., born 1914

Joe DiMaggio was the leading player of the New York Yankees when the team dominated American baseball in the 1930s and 1940s. Known as "Joltin' Joe" for his powerful hitting, DiMaggio joined the Yankees in 1936 and it was no accident that the club then won four World Series titles in a row. He played for the Yankees throughout his professional career (1936–51).

DiMaggio's most lasting personal achievement came in 1941 when he had at least one base hit in fifty-six consecutive games, a record that still stands unbeaten. After ending his run with a failure against the Cleveland Indians, DiMaggio then had another sixteen-game streak—an achievement in its own right. DiMaggio played centerfield and was also a star on his team's defense. It was said that he did not make a single error as a base runner in his whole career.

Joe DiMaggio finished his career with a .325 batting average and 361 home runs, and his slugging average of .579 stands sixth on the all-time list. In 1954, he was back in the headlines when he married and then divorced the famous movie star Marilyn Monroe.

▲ Joe DiMaggio at spring training.
▼ DiMaggio has another hit during his great spell in the 1941 season.

Lou Gehrig
U.S., 1903–41

Lou Gehrig was unquestionably one of baseball's all-time greats. His career was tragically cut short by illness, but he still set a batch of records that have proved to be among baseball's hardest to beat.

Lou Gehrig first got his chance with the New York Yankees in June 1925 when the regular first baseman was ill. Gehrig played in every Yankees game from that day until May 1939. His great fitness and durability earned him the nickname "Iron Horse," but he was a truly great hitter as well.

In the late 1920s and through the 1930s the Yankees had a truly great run with a team full of top stars. Some baseball fans think that the 1927 Yankees were the greatest team ever. But in that stellar lineup only "Babe" Ruth (see page 18) could stand comparison with Lou Gehrig.

Perhaps Gehrig's best personal year was 1934 when he won a Triple Crown—leading the American League in batting average (.363), RBI (165), and home runs (49). He led the league in RBI four more times and in home runs twice more. Even though his career was cut short, his lifetime total of runs batted in still stands at third in the all-time list.

> Lou Gehrig's career ended in 1939 when he took himself out of the Yankees' lineup because he realized that his strength and timing had deteriorated. He turned out to have a rare and incurable disease and died only two years later. Knowing that he was dying and reviewing his career, he said that he still thought he was "the luckiest man on the face of the Earth."

▶ Lou Gehrig, playing for the New York Yankees, crosses home plate on his home run in the ninth innings of the fourth World Series game on October 9, 1937.

Bob Gibson
U.S., born 1935

Bob Gibson was more than just one of baseball's greatest pitchers. He went to college on a basketball scholarship and played for a short time with the Harlem Globetrotters exhibition team. In baseball, too, he was more than just a strikeout specialist. He hit twenty-four home runs in the National League and in 1970 he even reached a batting average of .303.

Despite all this he is remembered most for his great pitching. Gibson only played for one major league club, the St Louis Cardinals. He joined them in 1959 and retired in 1975. Gibson was a fast and powerful righthander who could really dominate a game.

Fact File
Career strikeouts: 3,117
Career wins: 251
National League MVP: 1968
Cy Young Award: 1968, 1970
World Series titles (and MVP): 1964, 1967

His best season was 1968 when his earned run average was only 1.12. This was the best figure of modern times. Gibson pitched brilliantly in the 1968 World Series as well. He had thirty-five strikeouts, with seventeen in one game, but the Cardinals still lost to Detroit. Gibson could really turn on the style in the big games, though. The Cardinals took the World Series in 1964 and 1967 and both times he was named as Series MVP.

◀ Gibson pitching against the Boston Red Sox on October 12, 1967, in the final game of the World Series. He pitched the Cardinals to a 7–2 win.

Willie Mays
U.S., born 1931

Willie Mays was one of baseball's biggest stars of the 1950s and 1960s. He played center field for the Giants for most of his career. He joined the Giants from the Negro National League in 1950. He had a brief spell on a minor league farm team, but made his Giants debut in 1951. The Giants were then based in New York. Mays moved with them to San

▲ Willie Mays wearing the uniform of the San Francisco Giants in 1967.

◀ Mays takes a catch for the New York Giants.

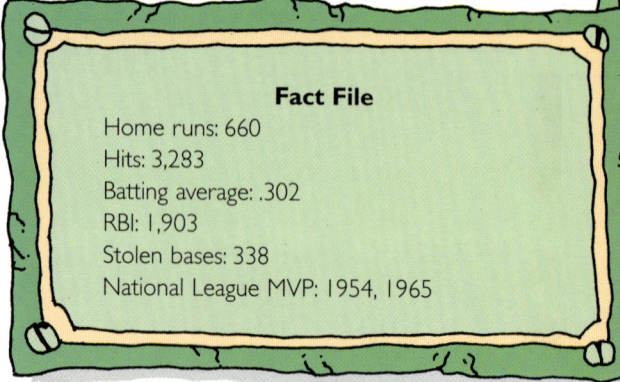

Fact File
Home runs: 660
Hits: 3,283
Batting average: .302
RBI: 1,903
Stolen bases: 338
National League MVP: 1954, 1965

Francisco in 1957 and stayed with the club until 1971. He finished his career in 1973 with the Mets.

Mays was a great power hitter. He led the National League in home runs four times. His career total of 660 home runs is the third best ever. He was also a fast and cunning base runner. He led the National League in stolen bases four times and seemed to have a special skill for making the most out of opponents' errors. He made very few mistakes in the field himself and used his great speed to make important catches and defensive plays.

Hideo Nomo
Japan, born 1968

Baseball has traditionally been regarded as America's favorite sport, with U.S. players and leagues considered the best in the world. However, baseball has gradually spread into Central and South America and across the Pacific Ocean, and now a Japanese player is making U.S. players and fans sit up and take notice.

Hideo Nomo began pitching in Japan's top league in 1990 with the Kintetsu Buffaloes and immediately proved that he would become a major star. He was not only acclaimed Rookie of the Year, but also added the prizes for best pitcher and most valuable player!

Sadaharu Oh
Nomo may develop into Japan's finest pitcher, but there is no doubt who was Japan's finest hitter. Sadaharu Oh (born 1940) led the Japan League in home runs fifteen times, hitting 868 in his 22-year career with the Yomiuri Giants. The U.S. record is Hank Aaron's 755.

In the first four seasons he had with Kintetsu, he had top of the league figures for games won, strikeouts and earned-run average. Then he decided to try his luck in the U.S., signing with the Los Angeles Dodgers. American baseball was looking for a new star in 1995 after the players' strike of 1994, and Nomo was the man. His pitching was so impressive that he was selected for the All-Star game in his first season. Even the best U.S. stars were bewildered by his unusual, twisting pitching action and the lightning-fast fastball that he produced.

◀ Hideo Nomo has an unusual pitching style producing an extremely fierce fastball.

Jackie Robinson
U.S., 1919–72

When Jackie Robinson stepped out for the first time with the Brooklyn Dodgers in April 1947, he was the first black player to appear regularly with any of baseball's top teams. Robinson attended the University of California at Los Angeles before World War II, and was a star of American football, baseball, basketball, and track and field (he was one of the world's best long-jumpers).

In 1946, he was signed by the Brooklyn Dodgers and made his major league debut a year later. Robinson had great strength of character, and this, together with his great playing skills, helped him in his fight against the racism that he encountered.

▲ Jackie Robinson during a season he spent with Montreal in the minor leagues before his breakthrough with the Dodgers.

▼ Jackie Robinson uses all his speed to slide safely into home base during a 1952 game with the Chicago Cubs. Robinson put his athletic talents to effective use as an outfielder as well.

In baseball's very first years, a number of black players played with the mainly white top teams. But from the 1880s, until Robinson's breakthrough, no black player played in the major leagues—instead, they played in what were called the "Negro Leagues." The players in the Negro Leagues were never paid as much as the white stars, but their talents were at least as impressive.

Pete Rose
U.S., 1941

Pete Rose set many baseball records in a long and distinguished playing career, Probably the most impressive feat was to amass 4,256 hits in his major league lifetime. This beat Ty Cobb's old record of 4,191 (see page 10) which many experts thought would stand for ever. After Rose retired from playing in 1986, however, he became a manager and in 1989 he was banned from baseball for life because of his involvement in betting on the game.

Rose was above all a great and versatile competitor. He was a switch hitter and played as both an outfielder and infielder. His nickname was "Charlie Hustle." His major league career began in 1963 with the Cincinnati Reds in 1963. Rose was one of the team's top players in the late 1960s and early 1970s when they were probably the strongest team in the National League. Rose himself won the National League batting title three times and was League MVP once.

Rose stayed with the Reds until 1978, but then played for the Philadelphia Phillies and finally the Montreal Expos before returning to the Reds shortly before the end of his career. He had become manager of the Reds when he was banned from the game.

Fact File
Pete Rose holds numerous major league records:
Number of games played: 3,562
Career hits: 4,256, 14,053 at bats
First to have over 200 hits in 10 different seasons
Number of straight 100-hit seasons: 23
National League MVP: 1973
National League batting titles: 1968, 1969, 1973

◀ Pete Rose batting for the Cincinnati Reds.

"Babe" Ruth
U.S., 1895–1948

"Babe" Ruth may have been baseball's finest ever player. Some of his records have been beaten in more recent years, but no one has come near his lifetime slugging average of .690. No other player has hit fifty home runs in more than two seasons—"the Babe" managed this four times. Most impressive of all, he hit home runs 8.5 percent of his times at bat.

George Herman Ruth was first called "the Babe" when he played for the Boston Red Sox. He had success as a pitcher with Boston and was also a powerful batter. He was traded to the New York Yankees in 1920. In his first season there he hit an amazing 54 home runs and soon switched to playing right field. He stayed with the Yankees, then baseball's strongest team, for most of his career which ran from 1914 to 1935.

▶ "Babe" Ruth practicing with the Boston Braves at the end of his career.

▼ "Babe" Ruth brought so many fans to baseball that Yankee Stadium was called "the house that Ruth built."

"Babe" Ruth hit baseball's most famous home run in the 1932 World Series. Coming up to bat for the Yankees in the third game, Ruth pointed at the farthest part of the fence, allowed two strikes to go past, then blasted the next into the crowd, exactly where he had shown he would.

Cy Young
U.S., 1867–1955

Cy Young played as a pitcher for the underdog Boston Red Sox in the first-ever World Series in 1903. During what was then a nine-game series, he won two games and helped his club to a shocking 5–3 win. Young, whose full name was Denton True Young, is remembered for much more than the part he played in the famous 1903 World Series.

From 1890 to 1911, he played with the Cleveland Spiders, St Louis Cardinals, Boston Red Sox and Cleveland Indians. In his remarkable career, he won 511 games, by a long way the best total ever. Only one other pitcher has won more than 400 games and no current player is near 300.

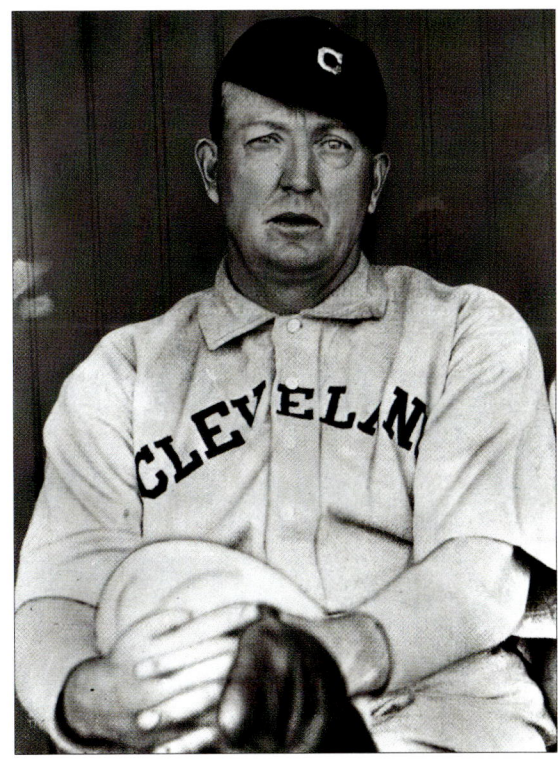

It is sometimes pointed out that Young lost more games than any other pitcher in the history of baseball —but his long career undoubtedly contributed to this fact. However, his game was consistently good: he won more than twenty games in twenty of his twenty-two seasons, and more than thirty games in five of the twenty seasons. With this record it is appropriate that the trophies awarded every year for the best pitchers in the two American baseball leagues are still known as the Cy Young awards.

◀ Cy Young warms up his pitching arm before another game in his long and successful career.

Professional baseball's two top leagues in North America are the National League (founded 1876) and the American League (founded 1901). The annual championship between the two leagues, called the World Series, was first played in 1903.

Kareem Abdul-Jabbar
U.S., born 1947

Kareem Abdul-Jabbar was one of the best centers ever to play the game. His trademark shot was his famous "sky hook," with which he won points from long range.

After starring in high school basketball in New York, Lew Alcindor, as he was then known, went on to UCLA and helped them win three consecutive NCAA championships.

Next, he was drafted by the Milwaukee Bucks, a weak team, made them title contenders in his first year and led them to the NBA championship in 1972. During this period he became a Muslim and changed his name. In 1976, Abdul-Jabbar moved to the Los Angeles Lakers and played there until 1989, winning the NBA title with the team five times.

Fact File
Height: 7 feet 2 inches
Points scored: 38,387 (5,762 in play-offs)—both best ever
Career points average: 24.6
MVP: 1971, 1972, 1974, 1976, 1977, 1980
All-American (UCLA): 1967–9

▼ Kareem Abdul-Jabbar in points scoring action in the familiar yellow uniform of the Los Angeles Lakers.

Larry Bird
U.S, born 1956

His critics said he was slow around the court and could not jump very well, but Larry Bird was still one of the greatest basketball forwards ever. He was a brilliant passer of the ball and had that special ability that helped the rest of his team play to their full potential.

At college he played for Indiana State, not normally a top team, and led them into the NCAA finals in his senior year when he was also named All-American for the second time.

When he turned professional in 1980, he was selected, or drafted, by the Boston Celtics and played with them for the whole of his career until his retirement in 1992. His peak was in the middle of the 1980s. He was named the National Basketball Association's (NBA's) Most Valuable Player in 1984 and 1986, and helped the Celtics to NBA championships in both of those years.

▲ Larry Bird scored 21,791 points for the Celtics in the course of his great career.

The "Dream Team"
For the first time in 1992, the U.S. Olympic basketball team was selected from the finest professional players in the NBA. Superstars, such as Michael Jordan and Magic Johnson, were on the team but Larry Bird was voted in as captain. The "Dream Team" won the gold medal, and after this success, Bird retired.

Bird was brought up in a small Indiana town called French Lick, and became known as "the hick from French Lick" ("hick" means "yokel"). Away from the basketball court, Bird remained a country boy at heart, but on court he had class and technique to spare.

▼ Larry Bird makes a drive for the basket, leaving an opponent stranded behind him.

Chicago Bulls
U.S., founded 1966

Before the mid-1980s, the Chicago Bulls had been one of the National Basketball Association's least successful teams. That began to change when they drafted Michael Jordan in 1983. Almost from the start, Jordan was a scoring sensation and the Bulls began to look like winners.

Real success began in 1991 when the Los Angeles Lakers were defeated 4–1 in the finals to give Chicago its first title. Repeat wins in 1992 over Portland and over Phoenix in 1993 showed that a basketball dynasty to rival the great teams of the past was being founded.

Then Jordan said that he was leaving to play baseball, and the Bulls slumped.

▲ Chicago coach Phil Jackson has one of the best records of any NBA coach ever.

In 1994 Jordan returned and in 1995 the Bulls reached the playoffs again, winning the NBA title in 1996.

▼ Muscle stretching is a vital part of athletic preparation as these Bulls show.

Winners in the NBA
The Chicago Bulls have a long way to go before their total of title wins catches up with basketball's most famous team of all, the Boston Celtics. The Celtics have won the championship sixteen times, including a period from 1957 to 1969 when they won eleven times in thirteen years.

"Magic" Johnson
U.S., born 1959

Earvin "Magic" Johnson was one of basketball's greatest stars throughout the 1980s. He joined the Los Angeles Lakers from the Michigan State Spartans in 1979, and soon showed the fans what he could do.

In his first season in 1980, he played in the NBA finals, and in the sixth and last game he played center instead of his usual position of point guard because Kareem Abdul-Jabbar was injured. "Magic" Johnson scored an astonishing forty-two points, fifteen rebounds and seven assists, and walked off the court with the playoffs' most valuable player (MVP) award.

Johnson was unusually tall for a guard at 6 feet 9 inches, but had great handling and passing skills. His performance in his first title series was one of many when he proved that he had the versatility to play in positions other than point guard. Throughout his career he played with

▲ "Magic" Johnson uses all his agility to get in a shot.

> Shortly before the start of the NBA season in 1991, "Magic" Johnson announced that he was retiring from the game and that he had been infected with HIV, the virus that leads to the disease AIDS. However, he played for the U.S. "Dream Team" in the 1992 Olympics, and since then has put his great popularity to work in the campaign against AIDS.

the Lakers, who were the best team in the basketball league in the 1980s, winning the NBA title five times and being finalists on three more occasions.

"Magic" Johnson was named as NBA MVP three times, in 1987, 1989 and 1990. His career total of 9,921 assists is the best ever, and shows that he was, above all, the sort of player who made his team play better.

◀ "Magic" Johnson celebrates the U.S.'s 1992 Olympic basketball gold medal.

Michael Jordan
U.S., born 1963

Michael Jordan is the greatest modern basketball player and probably the richest—he promotes many different sports products, especially for the Nike shoe company. Jordan was a noted player in college at North Carolina and a member of the 1984 U.S. Olympic gold-medal team. He was only taken as the third choice in the draft of players into the NBA, but once with the Chicago Bulls he almost instantly won recognition as the league's best scorer.

His points total in his first season (2,313) was the highest in the NBA, but his average let him down. After missing most of the next season with injury he won his first of seven successive scoring titles in 1986. Jordan's trademark was an ability seemingly to hang in the air and defy gravity, and he soon became known as "His Airness" to his many fans.

▲ The Lakers' defense cannot stop Jordan making another basket in the 1989–90 season.

From 1987 until 1993, he kept breaking records: highest career scoring average (32.3 points per game), most valuable player three times, defensive player of the year once and, best of all, gained three NBA titles with the Bulls from 1991 to 1993, and another in 1996.

In 1993 Jordan gave up basketball for more than a year in an unsuccessful attempt to develop a second career as a baseball player. He came back to basketball for the 1994–5 season, led the Bulls into the playoffs, and then in 1996 helped his team win a fourth NBA title.

◀ Michael Jordan takes to the air in another scoring demonstration of his uncanny leaping ability.

Cheryl Miller
U.S., born 1964

Cheryl Miller was the best female basketball player ever. Her list of awards and records is almost endless. Most of her notable achievements were as a college player with the University of Southern California. She led the team there to two U.S. national titles in 1983 and 1984, and was selected as the top player of the NCAA Final Four tournament in both of those winning years.

She won women's basketball's top trophy, the Naismith Award for the best player of the season, an unheard of three years in a row (1984–6), and in 1984 was voted as Collegiate Woman Athlete of the Year.

▲ The USC cheerleaders look on in admiration as Cheryl Miller demonstrates her skills.

▼ Cheryl Miller has no trouble rising above the hoop in this picture of her taken during a practice routine.

> Cheryl Miller is not the only top basketball player in her family. Her brother, Reggie Miller, is one of the stars of the NBA Indiana Pacers. He has not achieved the success of his sister, but is regularly his team's top scorer, and led the Pacers to the Eastern Conference Final in the playoffs in 1994.

In 1984 she played for the U.S. Olympic women's basketball team in the Olympic Games at Los Angeles. She was the star of the team that won the gold medal. She played for other U.S. national teams in 1986, as well as becoming first draft choice for a new professional women's basketball league. (This league was not a financial success and soon came to an end.) Cheryl Miller hoped to make the U.S. Olympic team in 1988, but injury brought her retirement.

Hakeem Olajuwon
Nigeria/U.S., born 1963

Hakeem Olajuwon is not the most outspoken of the current top basketball players, but he is certainly among the most talented and skillful. Nigerian by birth, he became a college star in the U.S. He was selected as All-American in 1984 and had been named MVP in the Final Four college tournament in 1983. It was no surprise he was the number one draft choice for the NBA in 1984 when he joined the Houston Rockets.

Olajuwon began to repay the Rockets' faith in him from his very first season when he was elected Rookie of the Year. He has been named to the All-NBA first team five times, the first time in 1987. Even better was to come in 1994 and

▶ Olajuwon jumps to shoot against the Pacers.

▼ Playing in a game early in 1995.

Fact File
Olajuwon's NBA titles
Rookie of the Year: 1984
Regular season MVP: 1994
Defensive Player of the Year: 1993, 1994
Top rebounder: 1989, 1990
Top shot blocker: 1990, 1991, 1993

1995 when he led the underdog Rockets to consecutive NBA titles.

In 1994, Olajuwon and his team beat the New York Knicks 4–3, and in 1995 they did it again the hard way. The Rockets came into the playoffs seeded only fifth after a modest season, but recaptured their best play to gain a finals place against Shaquille O'Neal's Orlando Magic. The confrontation between the NBA's two premier teams was one-sided, for Olajuwon and the Rockets ran away with the title 4–0.

Shaquille O'Neal
U.S., born 1972

As one of the superstars of the modern game of basketball, Shaquille O'Neal has a seven-year contract with the Orlando Magic which is worth $42,000,000.

O'Neal joined the Orlando Magic in the 1992 NBA draft after being twice selected as All-American in college. O'Neal's great scoring ability won him the award as NBA Rookie of the Year in 1993. In 1995, he finally gained his first top spot in the scoring race.

O'Neal's great weakness is his free-throw shooting. With a good free-throw percentage, O'Neal would be far ahead in the scoring statistics.

O'Neal is one of the best-known NBA stars for his off-court activities, but he also has the respect of the other stars. This was demonstrated when he was picked as part of the U.S.'s "Dream Team II," which won the 1994 World Championship (see page 19).

▼ Shaq O'Neal is a massive man. His playing position is center and he is 7 feet 1 inches tall and weighs 304 lb.

The Orlando Magic made the Eastern Conference final in the 1994–95 playoffs. Their regular season was distinguished by a great 39–2 record in front of their home fans, only one game short of the all-time NBA best. They returned to the playoffs in 1996.

CYCLING

Jeanne Longo
France, born 1958

Jeanne Longo is regarded as the finest all-round woman cycle racer ever. She was world road race champion from 1985 to 1987 and in 1989, pursuit champion in 1986, 1988 and 1989, and won the points title in 1989. In addition to these successes, she held both the road race and pursuit championships unbeaten from 1980 to 1989 in her home country of France. If she had any weakness it was in her sprinting speed.

Some cycling records are set with the help of a motorcycle—the cyclist rides close behind, which helps the rider to go at the correct pace—but the true records are set alone and from a standing start. In 1989, Longo established unaided records for 3 kilometers and one hour which are still unbeaten. Set at altitude in Mexico, her 1-hour ride was an astonishing 28.8 miles.

▲ Jeanne Longo during a pursuit race competition.

Her other successes include wins in the women's Tour de France in 1987, 1988 and 1989, and a silver medal in the road race at the 1992 Olympics.

▼ Longo in the yellow jersey of the race leader during the 1987 Tour de France which she won.

Miguel Indurain
Spain, born 1964

The Tour de France is the toughest race in the cycling world and one of the hardest in all sport. Miguel Indurain is the only person who has won it five years in succession (1991–95).

Indurain is not a great sprinter, but he is the finest time-trialler of his generation, building up huge leads over his opponents in these sections. Then he defends his times with astonishing power and determination in the mountain stages, where so many riders have their challenges broken.

Indurain competed for Spain in the 1984 Olympics as an amateur before turning professional the next year. Like many other riders, he dropped out of the race in his first two entries in the Tour de France, but gradually moved up

▲ Miguel Indurain showing all his power and determination during an attempt on the world 1-hour distance record in September 1994.

the rankings after that. He recorded his first stage win in 1989 when he was seventeenth overall.

As well as his Tour de France wins, he has also won the important Giro d'Italia race twice, and holds the 1-hour world record of 32.98 miles.

Each year as Indurain's reputation has grown the headlines in the cycling magazines have been, "Can anyone catch Indurain?" The answer so far has been a definite "no."

Indurain's Remarkable Physique
Indurain is tall for a top cyclist (6 feet 2 inches), but is a very powerful rider. His lung capacity has been measured at 3.39 cu. feet, twice that of a normal healthy adult man, and his resting heart beat is 28 per minute (compared with about 68 for the average man).

◀ Indurain in the familiar race leader's yellow jersey during the 1995 Tour de France. He is closely followed by one of his Banesto teammates.

Greg LeMond
U.S., born 1961

Californian Greg LeMond is America's greatest ever cycling star. He is the only American who has won cycling's toughest race, the Tour de France.

LeMond first got a spot in the headlines in the cycling world in 1979 when he won three gold medals in the world junior championships. This success set him up to turn professional in 1981. In 1982 he was one of the stars of the world road race championships, but he ended up having to settle for second place. In 1983 he really made his mark when he became world champion for the first time.

Cycling fans say that the real test of a racer's pace and determination comes in

> Greg LeMond achieved his fantastic cycling record even though he was nearly killed in a hunting accident. He was shot in the back and nearly died in 1986. People thought he would never race again, but he recovered well enough to win the Tour de France twice.

the Tour de France. LeMond rode in the Tour for the first time in 1984 and came in third—an amazing feat for a rookie.

In 1986 he did it. He came home with his first-ever Tour de France winner's yellow jersey. He won again in 1989 in one of the most exciting races ever. His winning margin after three weeks of racing was just 8 seconds. LeMond rounded out a great career with another world championship in 1989 and a third Tour de France win in 1990.

◀ LeMond winning the final stage of the 1989 Tour de France as he passes the Arc de Triomphe in Paris. The yellow jersey (*maillot jaune*) indicates that he was leading the race at the time.

Eddy Merckx
Belgium, born 1945

In cycling's great races, the leaders in the various categories of competition wear a distinctive colored jersey. Only Eddy Merckx has ever finished the Tour de France entitled to wear all three leaders' jerseys as overall winner, points champion and "King of the Mountains."

Merckx and three others have each won the Tour de France five times, but Merckx stands alone with thirty-five stage wins and ninety-six days as race leader. Merckx's wins were in 1969–72 and 1974. He also won the Giro d'Italia five times, and in 1974 was the first cyclist to win the three top races, the Tour de France, the Giro d'Italia and the world road race championship in the same year.

▲ Eddy Merckx in Tour de France action.

▼ Eddy Merckx crosses the finish line to win the 1971 world professional road race championship.

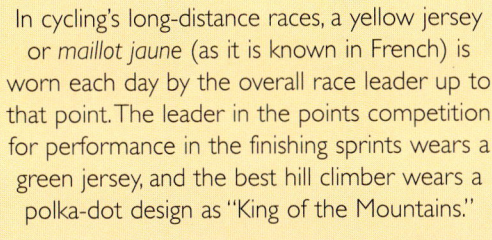

In cycling's long-distance races, a yellow jersey or *maillot jaune* (as it is known in French) is worn each day by the overall race leader up to that point. The leader in the points competition for performance in the finishing sprints wears a green jersey, and the best hill climber wears a polka-dot design as "King of the Mountains."

Jim Brown
U.S., born 1936

Jim Brown was the best fullback ever to play football, but some people think that this may not even have been his best sport. He played basketball at college and competed at top level in the decathlon, but lacrosse fans think he may have been the best all-round player ever in their game.

After twice being named All-American in college football, Brown was drafted in 1957 by the Cleveland Browns. He made Rookie of the Year and, in his second year (1958), set an incredible new record for rushing yards gained in the season, improving the old mark by more than one third. In his nine-year professional career, he led the league in rushing eight times, "failing" only in 1962, and never missed a single game because of injury.

The records he set are gradually being beaten by modern stars because of changes in the way the game is played. Even so, his career rushing yards total of 12,312 yards was only surpassed by Walter Payton in the 1980s. Brown's average gain per carry of the ball was 5.2 yards and this has yet to be beaten.

Fact File
Jim Brown: 6 feet 1 inch, 233 pounds
Syracuse University: All-American
National Football League career: 1957–65
Rushing record: 12,312 yards (average 5.2 yards), 106 touchdowns
Receiving: 2,499 yards (average 9.5 yards), 20 touchdowns

▶ To commemorate Jim Brown's achievements the Cleveland Browns retired his number 32 when he finished playing.

Dick Butkus
U.S., born 1942

Dick Butkus was a hard-hitting linebacker who was one of the toughest defenders in football history. Butkus was one of the linebackers named to the National Football League's All-Time Team on the league's 75th anniversary in 1994.

Butkus was born in Chicago and attended the University of Illinois. At college he was named to the All-American team in 1963 and 1964. He played center as well as linebacker in college and in 1964 he finished third in the voting for the Heisman Trophy given to the nation's best college player—an almost unequaled success for a defensive player or a lineman.

Dick Butkus was known throughout his football career for his tough-talking, no-nonsense attitude. But after his retirement from football Butkus showed another side to his character and developed a successful second career as a movie and television actor.

After college Butkus was drafted by the Chicago Bears. He played with the Bears for nine years and made All-Pro in seven of them. He only missed out in 1966 and in his final season before retirement in 1973 when he was hampered by the knee injuries that ended his career.

Butkus specialized in the middle linebacker position. He was mobile enough to make tackles and interceptions all round the field and he had the weight (245 lb) and power to make his hits really count.

◀ Butkus making a 6-yard gain in a game between the Bears and the Bengals in November 1972.

Dan Marino
U.S., born 1961

Dan Marino is one of the finest quarterbacks ever to play football. His great skills have been matched with strength and durability that have helped him return from numerous injuries and surgical operations to be as good as ever.

Dan Marino now holds the NFL all-time records in virtually all the categories of quarterback play. He beat Fran Tarkenton's previous record of 342 touchdowns and his figures for yards gained, number of completions and number of pass attempts all in the 1995 season. By the end of that season he had thrown for 352 touchdowns. In the summer of 1996 he signed a new three-year contract with the Miami Dolphins and will surely extend his lead at the top of the list even more.

Fact File
Height: 6 feet 4 inches; weight: 224 lb
Career passing yards: 48,841
Completions: 3,910
NFL career and single season record holder for passing TD, passing yards, completions
AFC leading passer: 1983, 1984, 1986, 1989
(figures to start of 1996 season)

Pittsburgh-born Marino was a star in high school and again at college with the University of Pittsburgh. Drafted in the first round by the Dolphins in 1983, he was Rookie of the Year and started in the Pro Bowl in his first season. The next year he set a clutch of NFL single-year records that still stand: 5,084 yards passing, 48 touchdown passes, 362 completions, and four 400-yard games.

◀ Dan Marino in action against the New York Giants in November 1990. He threw for 245 yards and two touchdowns to become the eleventh passer to pass the 30,000-yard mark.

Joe Montana
U.S., born 1956

Joe Montana was one of the greatest quarterbacks ever to play football. Montana began his big-time career with the Fighting Irish of Notre Dame, always one of the strongest of the U.S. college teams. His most famous game there was the 1979 Cotton Bowl, when he led the team from 34–12 down in the third quarter to a 35–34 win.

The scouts for the professional teams of the NFL thought he might be rather inconsistent, so he was only picked, or drafted, by the San Francisco 49ers in the third round, but he soon won a place in their starting line-up.

Overall, San Francisco was probably the strongest team in the NFL in the 1980s—thanks largely to Montana's leadership on the field. Montana soon became known as the most accurate

▲ Montana as a Kansas City Chief.

> A great quarterback needs to be matched with a great pass receiver if his talents are to be fully recognized. Montana's favorite partner for the second half of his career at San Francisco was Jerry Rice, perhaps the greatest wide receiver of all time (see page 38).

passing quarterback in the game with an uncanny ability to inspire his team to make great comebacks from apparently hopeless situations. Montana led the 49ers in four Super Bowl wins (1982, 1985, 1989 and 1990). Montana missed most of the 1991 and 1992 seasons because of injury. He retired in 1995 after two seasons with the Kansas City Chiefs.

◀ Montana in action in Super Bowl XXIII. The 49ers beat the Bengals 20–16.

Joe Namath
U.S., born 1943

Joe Namath is famed particularly for the great game at Super Bowl III (played on January 12, 1969), when he led the New York Jets to a stunning underdog victory over the powerful Baltimore Colts. Namath was chosen as the game's "most valuable player" (MVP) after this upset 16–7 win for the Jets.

Namath had joined the professional ranks in 1965 from the University of Alabama. He signed up for the Jets for $400,000, and quickly began to justify what was then a huge sum. In his first season, he passed for over 2,000 yards and was chosen as Rookie of the Year.

In 1967 he became the first professional quarterback to pass for more than 4,000 yards in a season; in 1968 he was chosen as his league's MVP.

▲ Joe Namath doing what he did best, making a big passing play, this time in a preseason Jets-Giants game in 1969.

The AFL and the NFL
When Joe Namath became a professional football player, two formerly rival leagues in American football, the American Football League (AFL) and the National Football League (NFL), had only recently joined together. The Jets were an AFL team and their win in Super Bowl III was the first ever by an AFL team.

Above all, Namath liked to pass the football. He probably had the strongest arm of any quarterback in football history, and he relished the challenge of going for the big plays. Touchdowns were his target, and he passed for 173 touchdowns in his professional career. Although he was hampered in the later years of his career by knee injuries, he played on until 1977, eventually gaining 27,663 yards as a passer from 1,886 pass completions.

◄ Joe Namath's great talent was recognized when he was elected to the Pro Football Hall of Fame in 1985.

Walter Payton
U.S., born 1954

Walter Payton was one of the finest running backs ever to play football. His records for the number of yards gained in rushing and for all-purpose yardage are likely to remain unbeaten for a very long time.

Payton was born in Columbia, Mississippi, and played college football with Jackson State University. Payton then joined the Chicago Bears in 1975 and played his entire NFL career with them until he retired in 1987. He was not a big man by NFL standards, but was exceptionally strong. He also had great balance and speed and the vision to find holes in the defense that most players would never have seen.

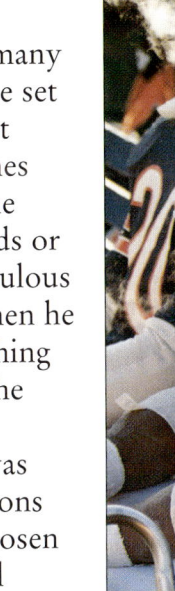

Among the many NFL records he set was the greatest number of games (77) in which he gained 100 yards or more and a fabulous day in 1977 when he gained 275 rushing yards against the Vikings. That performance was one of the reasons why he was chosen as the National Football League's MVP in 1977. Payton was one of the team leaders in the Bears's triumph in Super Bowl XX in 1986.

▼ Walter Payton making yardage in the second quarter of the game in which he broke Jim Brown's rushing record of 12,312 yards (see page 32). The game was between the Chicago Bears and the New Orleans Saints and was played on October 7, 1984.

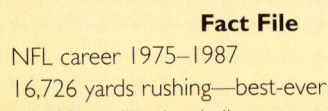

Fact File
NFL career 1975–1987
16,726 yards rushing—best-ever
21,803 yards gained all-purpose—best-ever
1,000 yards rushing in ten of thirteen seasons
Named All-Pro seven times

Jerry Rice
U.S., born 1962

Jerry Rice of the San Francisco 49ers is the greatest wide receiver in the history of pro football. San Francisco picked him from Mississippi Valley State in the first round of the 1985 draft and has never regretted that choice.

Rice immediately formed one of the game's greatest partnerships with the 49ers quarterback genius Joe Montana (see page 35). Together they led the 49ers to glory in the late 1980s. Rice was named the National Football League's MVP in 1987. Rice was Super Bowl MVP in 1989 when San Francisco thrashed Denver 55–10.

After Montana left San Francisco, Rice continued to notch records. He became the NFL's all-time touchdown leader in one of the first games of the 1994 season, beating Jim Brown's long-standing mark of 126.

By the start of the 1996 season, Rice had moved this record on to 156—a standard that will surely remain unbeaten for a very long time. Jerry Rice has it all—super speed, great hands, and the concentration and determination to put these to use. The records he leaves behind when he finally retires will be tough ones to crack.

> **Fact File**
> 156 career touchdowns; 942 receptions
> Best game: 5 TDs against Atlanta in 1990
> Best season: 22 TDs in 1987 (NFL record)
> Best season yardage: 1,848 yards in 1995 (NFL record)
> (To start of 1996 season)

◀ Jerry Rice is hit by a San Diego Charger cornerback, as he catches a touchdown pass in the third quarter of Super Bowl XXIX on January 29, 1995. Rice scored three touchdowns in the game.

Deion Sanders
U.S., born 1967

Deion "Prime Time" Sanders is one of the most talented and versatile athletes in American sports today. He has now given up his baseball career, but is still one of a very few top football players who plays at the highest level both on offense and defense.

Sanders joined the Atlanta Falcons in 1989 after he had twice been voted All-American during his college career at Florida State. He had been one of the finest ever defensive backs in college football and has since gained equally high honors in the pro game. At Atlanta he was named All-Pro three seasons in a row. He then joined San Francisco in 1994 as a free agent and helped them to a Super Bowl triumph at the end of that season. In the 1995 season he moved on once again, this time to the Dallas Cowboys. It was a smart move because Dallas was on its way to winning Super Bowl XXX, with Sanders as one of the team stars.

Sanders usually features in the cornerback position on defense, but he has also made big plays on offense in the pros as kick returner and wide receiver.

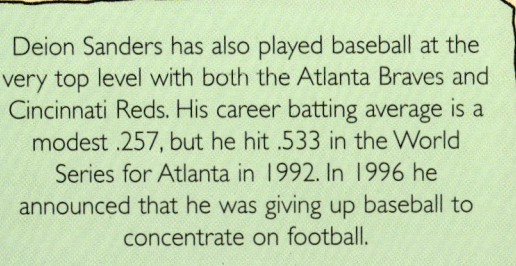

▲ Sanders celebrates with the Vince Lombardi trophy after the Cowboys beat the Steelers 27–17 in Super Bowl XXX.

▼ Sanders tries to catch a pass against the San Diego Chargers in Super Bowl XXIX.

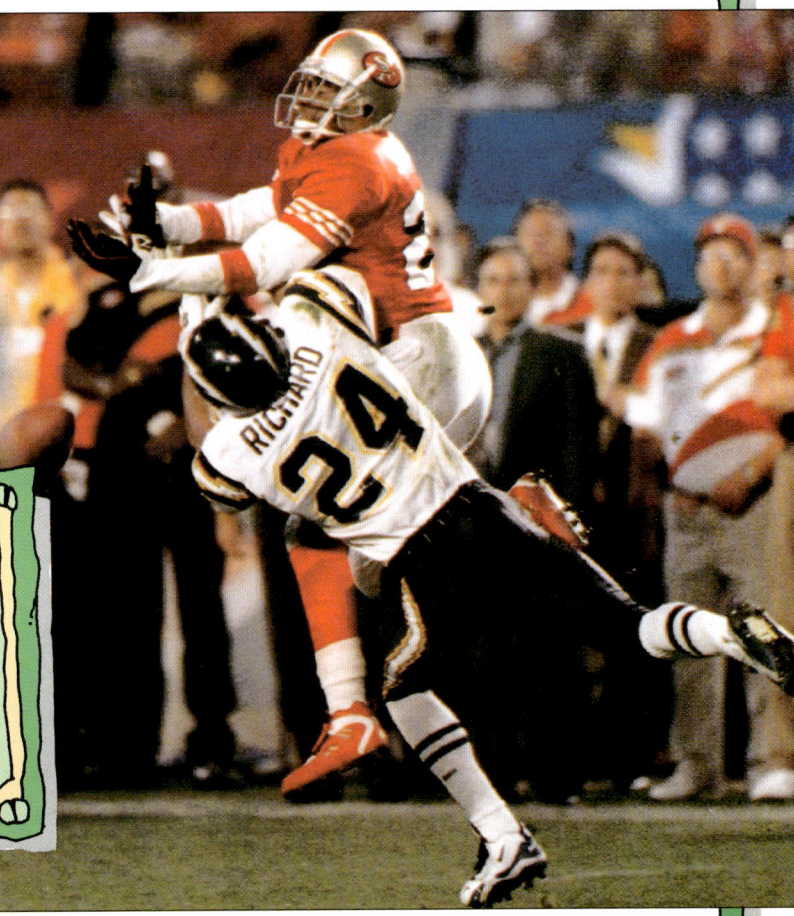

Deion Sanders has also played baseball at the very top level with both the Atlanta Braves and Cincinnati Reds. His career batting average is a modest .257, but he hit .533 in the World Series for Atlanta in 1992. In 1996 he announced that he was giving up baseball to concentrate on football.

Emmit Smith
U.S., born 1969

The Dallas Cowboys have been football's strongest team in the 1990s and at the heart of their success has been running back Emmit Smith. In just six years of NFL stardom, to the end of the 1995 season, Smith racked up ninety-six rushing touchdowns, well in sight of Walter Payton's all-time mark of 110.

Smith played his college ball at Florida and entered the NFL draft in his junior year in 1990. He had already been named All-American and the Cowboys picked him in the first round. He was a star from the moment he pulled on the Cowboys uniform. He ran for 937 yards and the Rookie of the Year spot in 1990 and every season since he has topped the 1,400-yard mark, the only player ever to do so. His 1995 total of 1,773 yards is his best yet and was accompanied by twenty-five touchdowns (an NFL record).

Even better for the Cowboys is the fact that when Smith plays well they seldom lose. His greatest Cowboys game was probably in Super Bowl XXVIII when he was chosen MVP after the Cowboys' 30–15 win over Buffalo.

▼ Emmit Smith celebrates a 60-yard touchdown run against the New York Giants in September 1995.

Fact File
Height: 5 feet 9 inches; weight: 203 lb
Position: running back
NFL rushing leader: 1991, 1992, 1993, 1995
Best season: 1,773 yards, 25 TD in 1995
(To start of 1996 season)

Jim Thorpe
U.S., 1888–1953

Jim Thorpe is the only man ever to have won both the decathlon and the pentathlon at the Olympic Games—a feat that will never be repeated. This triumph came in the 1912 Olympics held at Stockholm in Sweden. To make these wins even more impressive, he set world records in both events. A year later his gold medals were taken away because he had been paid $15 a week for playing baseball earlier in his career, and being paid for playing any sport was then against the rules of track and field.

Thorpe's ancestry was part Native American and his college was Carlisle Indian School, where he was coached by one of football's greatest coaches, Pop Warner. Thorpe was a football All-American in 1911 and 1912 at college, as well as starring at track and field.

Jim Thorpe's Olympic Medals
Jim Thorpe's family never stopped thinking that his medals had been taken away unfairly. Finally, in 1982, the International Olympic Committee agreed, and one of Thorpe's daughters was presented with replicas of the trophies which her father had deservedly won seventy years before.

From 1913 to 1919, he played pro baseball for the New York Giants, Boston Braves and Cincinnati Reds.

He also played professional football with the Canton Bulldogs, one of the top teams at that time. In 1920, he helped the Bulldogs join a new football league that eventually became the forerunner of the modern NFL. The Bulldogs became the Cleveland Indians in 1921 and Thorpe played with them and other teams until his career ended with the Chicago Cardinals in 1928.

▲◄ Jim Thorpe was one of the truly great and truly versatile athletes. Here he is seen (top) with the New York Giants and (left) with the Canton Bulldogs.

Seve Ballesteros
Spain, born 1957

During the 1980s, the U.S.'s domination of the world of golf was threatened by Europe, and at the head of the challenge was Spain's finest ever player, Severiano Ballesteros.

Ballesteros has always been exciting to watch. Sometimes his great power and attacking style go wildly wrong. But when this happens he treats the crowd to an exhibition of great recovery shots, playing impossibly delicate chips from the worst of lies and somehow walking away with birdies.

Ballesteros won five major championships during the 1980s (three British Opens and two U.S. Masters), and he is still capable of adding to that score.

▼ The full, high follow-through that completes Seve Ballesteros's golf swing shows the power that he puts into his shots.

Golf's most famous team competition is the Ryder Cup, which is held every two years between teams of the best U.S. and European professionals. Ballesteros was the inspiration for the European win in 1985 in Britain, followed by the first-ever European success in the U.S. in 1987.

Ben Hogan
U.S., born 1912

Ben Hogan was one of golf's greatest ever stars and even more remarkably he recorded most of his finest wins after he had been left virtually for dead in an automobile accident.

In February 1949, Hogan and his wife were driving home from a tournament when their car was crushed by a bus. Hogan threw himself across the seat to try and protect his wife from the impact. He managed to do so, but was so badly hurt himself that doctors thought he would die. No one thought he would ever be able to play golf again and certainly no one dreamed that he would ever compete again at the top level.

But Hogan was one of the hardest-working players ever and set to work with all his determination to make a comeback. When the time came for the 1950 U.S. Open, all golf fans were rooting for him. They were not to be disappointed. He led the tournament only to drop strokes over the last few regular holes. He had to settle for a spot in a three-way playoff, but his fighting spirit did not let him down and he finally won by four shots.

His greatest year was 1953 when he won three of golf's four professional majors—the closest anyone has ever come to repeating Bobby Jones's famous "Grand Slam" of 1930.

Fact File
USPGA tournament wins: 63
U.S. Open: 1948, 1950, 1951, 1953
U.S. PGA: 1946, 1948
U.S. Masters: 1951, 1953
British Open 1953
USPGA Player of Year 4 times, leading money winner 5 times

◀ Hogan blazes his way out of the rough near the fourteenth hole in the final round of the 1951 U.S. Open Championship. Playing in Birmingham, Michigan, Hogan described this as "the finest round I ever played."

Bobby Jones
U.S., 1902–71

Bobby Jones was one the world's greatest ever golfers. He is the only man to have won a "Grand Slam" of the four top tournaments in a single year.

Bobby Jones played his best golf in the 1920s when many of the top players, including himself, were amateurs. From 1923 to 1929 he won eight of what were then golf's biggest championships. But, while he was doing this, he was not even a full-time golfer!

In 1930, he concentrated on his golf and established a record that may well never be matched. He began by winning the British Amateur at St Andrews and then won both the British and U.S. Opens before finishing his Grand Slam in triumph in the U.S. Amateur at Merion in Pennsylvania.

▶ ▼ Two pictures of Bobby Jones on the way to winning the 1927 British Open, one of his thirteen major championship successes.

Jones and the Masters
Jones's lasting legacy to golf was in establishing the U.S. Masters tournament in 1934, held every year at the beautiful Augusta National Course. The winner of the Masters receives an unusual trophy, a special green jacket, presented each year by the defending champion from the year before.

Nancy Lopez
U.S., born 1957

There have been times in the history of women's golf when the skills of its players have not received the attention they deserve. Nowadays, the game is very healthy and much of that success is owed to the influence of Nancy Lopez.

If there has been one thing missing in Lopez's distinguished playing career it has been a win in the U.S. Ladies Open. She has had far more success in another major championship, the Ladies Professional Golfers Association or LPGA, which she won in 1978, 1985 and 1989.

Lopez's great contribution to women's golf was recognized by her election to the Golfing Hall of Fame in 1987, as soon as she was eligible.

▼ The grassy divots fly up, but Nancy Lopez's ball has long gone as she fires another approach shot into the heart of the green.

The Women's "Majors"
Like men's professional golf, the women's scene has four tournaments regarded as the most important. These are the U.S. Open, the U.S. LPGA Championship, the Nabisco Dinah Shore, and the du Maurier Classic. No player has yet won a "Grand Slam" of all four.

Jack Nicklaus
U.S., born 1940

Jack Nicklaus is considered to be the world's best-ever golfer. He took up the game when he was ten years old and scored 51 for his first nine holes. When he was thirteen, he played a round in 69 shots, so it was obvious even then that he was going to be very good.

"Big Jack" and "the Golden Bear" were Nicklaus's nicknames. He was known for his very long hitting, but his real championship-winning qualities were his fierce concentration and determination to win.

Golf has four major championships—the U.S. Open, the U.S. PGA, the U.S. Masters and the British Open—which are played every year. Since his first success in the 1962 U.S. Open, Nicklaus has won a major professional championship eighteen times, better than any other player ever. It is a record that will probably never be beaten.

Nicklaus is still winning a lot of money on the U.S. Seniors' Tour and continues to compete in some of the major tournaments on the regular professional circuit.

Fact File
Major Championship Wins: 18 (the most ever)
U.S. Open 1962, 1967, 1972, 1980
U.S. PGA 1963, 1971, 1973, 1975, 1980
U.S. Masters 1963, 1965, 1966, 1972, 1975, 1986
British Open 1966, 1970, 1978
Other Tournaments: U.S. Amateur 1959, 1961
Leading money winner in U.S. PGA tour 8 times

◀ By the look on Big Jack's face, this is one putt that did not go in the hole, from the 1980 British Open at Muirfield, won by Tom Watson.

Greg Norman
Australia, born 1955

Greg Norman is Australia's best-ever golfer, and has been one of the sport's biggest stars in the 1980s and 1990s.

Norman has had a great career, winning the British Open twice among sixty-plus tournament wins worldwide. Among all the successes there have been heartbreaks too. Four times Norman has lost in playoffs in the major championships.

Norman is accordingly known by two very different nicknames. To his fans he is known as the "Great White Shark." Others call him the "Great White Flag" for the number of times when he has, they say, given up when he could have won a big tournament. However he is still up at the top of the rankings and still challenging for the big prizes.

▼ Greg Norman won the British Open at Turnberry in 1986. The lighthouse beside the course's ninth tee is one of its best-known landmarks.

Norman's first British Open win was achieved at the Turnberry course in Scotland in 1986 when he alone coped well with difficult windy conditions. In 1993 at St George's in southern England, the fine weather made low scoring easier and Norman produced the Open's lowest ever total score of 267.

Arnold Palmer
U.S., born 1929

Arnold Palmer was golf's first superstar. His attacking style brought him a host of adoring fans, "Arnie's Army," and won him many tournaments with dramatic come-from-behind victories.

Palmer turned professional after winning the 1954 U.S. Amateur Championship. His best win was in the 1960 U.S. Open, played at Cherry Hills in Denver. Palmer was seven shots behind the leader after the third round, but had a round of 65 on the last afternoon to win by two strokes.

Palmer was the first golfer to win over $1 million in his career. This was a fitting achievement as it was his skill and personality that had made golf into a top international sport.

The End of an Era
Great rivals and friends, Arnold Palmer and Jack Nicklaus both decided that the 1995 British Open would be their last. Fittingly, it was held at St Andrews in Scotland, the home of golf, where both had previously recorded great British Open wins.

▲▼ Arnold Palmer's attacking play meant that he often had to get out of trouble—which he did with style. The pictures above and below were taken at the Masters tournament which he won four times.

Nick Price
Zimbabwe, born 1957

From time to time in every sport a player appears who is universally regarded as the best in the world. In the mid-1990s one modest Zimbabwean emerged as the best golfer in the world.

Nick Price started the 1990s near the top of the world rankings, but was not yet a superstar. He had a fine win in the U.S. PGA in 1992. In 1993 he topped the money list on the U.S. Tour, and 1994 was better still. He again led the money winners on the U.S. Tour with five first place finishes, and these included another PGA win.

Earlier in the year he had come to the British Open and produced a brilliant finish to snatch a prize he had come close to gaining twice before.

The 1994 Majors
The 1994 season was the first time ever that none of golf's four biggest tournaments was won by an American.
In addition to Price's two wins, South Africa's Ernie Els won the U.S. Open and Spain's José Maria Olazabal won the U.S. Masters.

▼ Nick Price hits his drive at probably the most famous hole in golf, the eighteenth at the Old Course at St Andrews, the traditional home of the game in Scotland. The historic Royal and Ancient clubhouse is in the background.

Patty Sheehan
U.S., born 1956

Patty Sheehan has been one of the biggest names in women's golf throughout the 1980s and 1990s.

Born in Vermont, Patty Sheehan is not only a great player, but also a lively competitor who makes the game fun for the spectators. She turned professional in 1980 after being one of the stars of the winning U.S. Curtis Cup team earlier that year. The professionals soon discovered that she could really play. She was voted Rookie of the Year in her debut season. Her second year was marked by her first win in a major tournament when she took the U.S.

▲ Patty Sheehan chips up to the eighteenth green in the Du Maurier Classic in August 1992.

◀ Sheehan winning a sudden-death playoff in Japan.

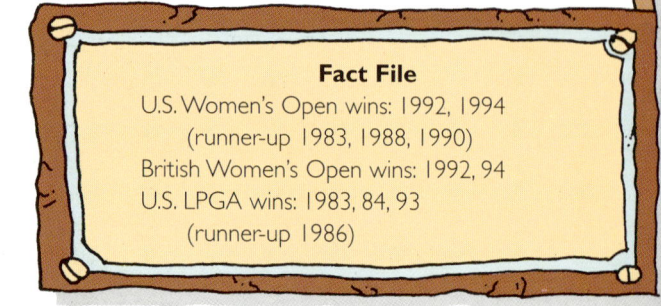

Fact File
U.S. Women's Open wins: 1992, 1994
(runner-up 1983, 1988, 1990)
British Women's Open wins: 1992, 94
U.S. LPGA wins: 1983, 84, 93
(runner-up 1986)

Women's Open. In her third year, 1983, she added a second major win, the U.S. LPGA, and was named Player of the Year on the tour.

Since then she has added numerous other tournament wins in the U.S. and British opens, the U.S. LPGA and other events. She has also been a leading member of U.S. Solheim Cup teams in their matches against the European professionals. Her great contribution to women's golf was finally recognized when she was made a member of the LPGA Hall of Fame in 1993.

Nikolai Andrianov
USSR, born 1952

Nikolai Andrianov holds the record number of Olympic medals of any man in any sport. His total of fifteen (seven gold, five silver and three bronze) was achieved in 1972, 1976 and 1980.

Andrianov's best discipline in the range of skills that make up gymnastics competitions was the rings exercise, where he had the special combination of power and seemingly effortless control that marks a true champion. He was twice world champion on the rings in 1974 and 1978, but won the Olympic gold at this event only once in 1976, as compared with his two golds each for the floor exercises and vault.

Andrianov first came to international notice in the 1971 European championships, in which he achieved third place overall. The 1976 Olympics was clearly his best competitive performance. He won the individual all-around title to add to his three other golds in the apparatus sections.

> **Men's Gymnastic Competitions**
> Theoretically it is possible for a male gymnast to win eight medals in a single major competition. Male gymnasts compete in six different exercises, plus the individual and team all-around titles. The six exercises are: horizontal bar, parallel bars, vault, pommel horse, rings, and floor exercise.

▶ Nikolai Andrianov on the way to winning the gold medal for the rings exercise at the 1976 Olympic Games in Montreal. He manages to look fairly relaxed despite the great power needed to achieve perfect balance in this position.

Vera Càslàvska
Czechoslovakia, born 1942

Vera Càslàvska was the leading women's gymnast at both the 1964 and 1968 Olympics. She holds second place in the list of all-time women Olympic medal winners with a total of seven golds and four silvers.

Càslàvska's first Olympics was in 1960 when she took a silver medal with the Czech team. She won a gold medal for the vault at the 1962 world championships, and traveled to the 1964 Tokyo Olympics as one of the favorites for the gymnastics competition. She did not disappoint her fans, beating the previous champion, Larissa Latynina, into second place in the competition for the all-round title, and winning two individual golds in the vault and beam.

In the 1968 Olympics, Càslàvska also won three individual golds (in the all-round competition, asymmetric bars and floor). This was especially brave because Czechoslovakia, her home country, had just been invaded by the then USSR and Càslàvska was a strong supporter of the government that had been overturned by the communists. She even had to do some of her training while she was in hiding for fear of being arrested.

▼ Vera Càslàvska pauses beautifully to show off her grace and balance during a beam exercise competition.

> Càslàvska shared the gold medal for the floor exercises at the 1968 Mexico Olympics with a Soviet athlete, Larissa Petrik, but there was no doubt who won the hearts of the crowd. Càslàvska chose to perform her routine to the music of the Mexican Hat Dance, which helped to endear her to the fans in Mexico City.

Nadia Comaneci
Romania, born 1961

Standards and records in most sports are usually gradually improved or beaten, but some of Nadia Comaneci's performances can never be bettered because they were judged to be absolutely perfect.

Gymnastics had begun to be made really popular with the charming skills displayed by the Russian gymnast Olga Korbut at the 1972 Olympics, but it was not until Comaneci came to the Montreal Olympics in 1976 that the sport truly took off.

Her flying, tumbling performances on the asymmetric (uneven) parallel bars and on the beam apparatus captured the hearts of the watching world. She was awarded a total of seven perfect scores of ten and came home with three gold medals. She was the first person ever to achieve a perfect score in gymnastics.

▲ After her stunning performance in 1976, Nadia won many other competitions, including two more Olympic gold medals in 1980.

When Comaneci won her first Olympic titles, she was 14 years old, stood 4 feet 11 inches tall and weighed 86 lb. By 1980 she had grown to 5 feet 3 inches and weighed 106 lb. It says much for her determination that she was still able to compete and win, despite the changes that had taken place in her physique.

Larissa Latynina
USSR, born 1934

Larissa Latynina was one of the finest ever gymnasts. She performed at a time when female gymnasts concentrated more on balletlike grace of movement rather than the tumbling moves that have become fashionable in recent years.

Latynina had originally trained as a ballet dancer and this was most clearly seen in the floor exercises element of her gymnastics routines. She won the floor exercises in each Olympics at which she competed (1956, 1960 and 1964).

In world and Olympic gymnastic competitions, Latynina won more gold medals than any other competitor. Altogether her medals totaled twelve individual and five team golds, as well as nine silvers and five bronzes. Her total of eighteen Olympic medals is also a record for any competitor (man or woman) in any sport.

▲ Larissa Latynina performs her floor exercises routine during the 1960 Olympic Games in Rome. Her performance was good enough to win the gold medal.

◄ In 1964 in Tokyo Latynina starred in the floor exercises and took gold once more.

Fact File
Latynina's Olympic gold medals:
1956: all-around, floor, vault and team
1960: all-around, floor and team
1964: floor and team (silver in the all-around competition)

Montreal Canadiens
Canada, founded 1909

Only two of the teams that were part of the National Hockey League (NHL) when it was formed in 1917 are still playing today, the Toronto Maple Leafs (first known as the Toronto Arenas) and the sport's most successful team ever, the Montreal Canadiens.

The Canadiens first began to delight fans in their hockey-mad city in 1909, when they played in what was then known as the National Hockey Association. In 1917, the team won its first major trophy, the Stanley Cup, in a playoff with the champions of the then operating Pacific Coast Hockey Association.

Since the formation of the NHL, the Canadiens have put their name on its top trophy another twenty-three times, almost twice as many times as their closest rivals. Their greatest years were from the mid-1950s through the 1970s, when they won the championship an amazing fifteen times.

The Canadiens' great players have included the brilliant but volatile Maurice "Rocket" Richard and, throughout the 1970s successes, the speedy sharpshooter Guy La Fleur.

▼ The Canadiens' familiar red uniforms lead the chase for the puck in this 1992 game with the Chicago Blackhawks.

> The Canadiens' first sight of glory after they joined the NHL came in the Stanley Cup finals in 1919, but this ended disappointingly when, with the series tied, it had to be abandoned because of a flu epidemic. This is the only time since it was established in 1893 that the Stanley Cup has not been won.

Wayne Gretzky
Canada, born 1961

Wayne Gretzky is known simply to ice hockey fans as "The Great One." Gretzky first made his mark in the 1979–80 season when he became the youngest player ever to be top scorer in the NHL. From then until the present, the records have continued to be broken —more than sixty at the last count.

In the 1980s, he won at least one of the game's top individual trophies every year, and from 1980 to 1985 he won and retained both the Hart Trophy as the league's MVP and the Ross Trophy as top points scorer.

The crowning moment came in March 1994 when he scored his 802nd goal, passing Gordie Howe's long-standing NHL record.

▶ ▼ Both pictures show Wayne Gretzky in action with the Los Angeles Kings whom he joined in 1988. As a professional he first played briefly for the Indianapolis Racers and from 1979–88 for the Edmonton Oilers.

Despite all his scoring records, Gretzky does not think of himself as a particularly great goal scorer. Nor does he have unique power or pace on the ice. Instead, Gretzky would prefer to be remembered for his play-making skills and ability to read the game which, to most fans, are simply the best ever.

Gordie Howe
Canada, born 1928

Professional ice hockey is a fast, furious and tough sport, and no place for anyone who cannot look after themselves. One man is a legend for setting records in five decades with an active professional career of thirty-two years and over 2,000 games.

Gordie Howe joined the Detroit Red Wings in the U.S. National Hockey League (NHL) in 1946 when he was aged nineteen, and he did not finally hang up his skates and retire for good until 1980 when he left the Hartford Whalers at the age of fifty-one.

Howe was a big man, 6 feet 4 inches tall and weighing 205 lb, but he matched his size with speed around the ice and very impressive hockey stick-handling skills.

Most of the NHL records he set have since been overtaken by the astonishing Wayne Gretzky. However, if his 1970s career in the World Hockey Association is included, Howe is still far ahead with 2,358 career points, including 975 goals.

▼ The hair may have been gray (or at least what was left of it), but Gordie Howe was still quick enough to win the puck and score in this game in his last season.

All in the Family
It is quite common for brothers or sisters to play together at the highest levels of sport. However, when Howe made his comeback with Houston in 1973, he achieved a rather different distinction, joining his sons Marty and Mark on the team.

Sven Tumba
Sweden, born 1931

The Swedes, like the Canadians, are crazy about ice hockey and Sven Tumba was one of their greatest-ever stars.

He also represented his country in soccer (in five internationals) and golf, even though he only took up playing golf seriously after his long ice hockey career was over. He played for Sweden in golf's 1974 World Cup.

As an ice hockey player, he led the Swedish team for most of the 1950s and 1960s. He won Olympic medals with the team in 1952 and 1964. Sweden also won the World Championship in 1953, 1957 and 1962.

▶ Tumba (center) at the World Championships at Tammerfors in 1965.

▼ Tumba celebrates a goal against Canada during the 1965 World Championships.

The oddest thing about Sven Tumba was that his real name was Sven Johansson. He became so famous that he started to be called Tumba after the suburb of Stockholm where he lived as a child.

Bonnie Blair
U.S., born 1964

The attention of most ice skating fans at the 1994 Winter Olympics was concentrated on the headline-grabbing quarrel between U.S.'s Tonya Harding and Nancy Kerrigan. However, while all that was going on, Bonnie Blair earned a place in the record books for her performances on the ice, not her activities off it.

Blair first won a place on the U.S. Olympic speed skating team in 1984, but did not figure in the medals in those games. In 1986, she set her first-ever world record over 500 meters on the 111-meters "short track," and followed this up with a 500-meters "long track" record the next year (the "long" or standard track is 400 meters to a lap).

Blair's first Olympic win came in the 500 meters in the 1988 Games, and the time she set in her gold-medal performance, after an especially quick start, remains the Olympic record. She also won bronze in the 1,000 meter race.

At the 1992 and 1994 Winter Olympics, she was at the top of her form winning both the sprints in both games. Blair has also won other important competitions including the 1994 World Cup at both her distances.

America's Finest—Blair or Heiden?
Before Blair, America's best-ever speed skater was unquestionably Eric Heiden. Both have won five Olympic golds, but on a strict medal count Blair comes out on top because of the single bronze medal she gained in 1988.

◀ Bonnie Blair in training in 1991 showing all the concentration and determination that have made her such a great champion.

Irina Rodnina
USSR, born 1949

Irina Rodnina has the greatest-ever competitive record of any figure skater. Her event was the pairs skating and she recorded her record number of medal-winning performances amazingly with two different partners, first Aleksei Ulanov and then Aleksandr Zaitsev.

Rodnina won ten successive World Championships from 1969 to 1978. For the first four she was with Ulanov and the remainder with Zaitsev.

Rodnina and Ulanov also won the gold medal at the 1972 Olympics, but then she began competing with Zaitsev, whom she married in 1976.

Rodnina remained undefeated in the European, World and Olympic championships with Zaitsev from 1973 to 1978, and added a third Olympic title to her list in 1980. She only missed out in 1979 because she took time off to have their baby.

▲ In pairs skating, the competitors must have strength and timing for the lifts and jumps....

▼ ... and grace and elegance for the dance sections.

The Perfect Score
Zaitsev was probably the better partner for Rodnina, on the ice as well as off it, because together they achieved a completely perfect score at the 1973 European Championships, gaining marks of six from all twelve judges.

Torvill & Dean
Great Britain

Jayne Torvill and Christopher Dean have been perhaps the finest ever exponents of the graceful and stylish art of ice dancing. They came in fifth in the 1980 Olympics and then their great days really began. They won four successive World Championships from 1981 to 1984, each time producing superbly arranged and beautifully executed new routines in the original and free dance sections.

Their *Barnum* routine won them nine maximum six scores for artistic interpretation at the 1983 World Championships. However, their finest routine of all was undoubtedly their stunning interpretation of Ravel's *Bolero*, which they produced for the 1984 Olympics and World Championships, both of which they won.

In the World Championships, they received thirteen maximum marks out of a possible eighteen, the best ice dance performance ever.

They then turned professional and toured very successfully with their own ice show, but were allowed to return to international competition in the 1994 Olympics. Their 1994 season started well when they won the European Championship. Then, sadly, the dream of Olympic gold went wrong when part of their routine was judged to include illegal moves. The marks lost meant they had to settle for the bronze medal.

> The figure skating competition at the Winter Olympics always concludes with a gala evening at which the medal winners perform their best routines.
> In 1994 Torvill and Dean chose their famous *Bolero* programme as their party piece and left the Olympics to a roar of applause.

◀ In training for the 1994 Olympics. Fans may have thought that Torvill and Dean were as good as ever, but the judges disagreed.

Bjørn Dæhlie
Norway, born 1967

Bjørn Dæhlie is joint top of the Winter Olympics all-time gold medal winning table, and his three silvers in addition to his five golds place him second on the list of winners of all types of medal.

Dæhlie has been a star at the last two Winter Olympic Games in 1992 and 1994. At the 1992 Olympics, Dæhlie won his first three golds in the 15-kilometer freestyle pursuit, 50-kilometer classical and in the relay with the Norwegian team.

In 1994, he again won four medals, this time two golds and two silvers. The relay race in which Dæhlie was second was probably the most dramatic event of the whole 1994 games.

Norway's team headed the medal table at the 1994 Winter Olympics with the two biggest individual contributions coming from Dæhlie and speed skater Johann Olav Koss, who won three golds in the 1,500 meters, 5,000 meters and 10,000 meters. Like Dæhlie, Koss had also been a star and medal winner at the 1992 Games.

▲ Bjørn Dæhlie strides out to win one of his great collection of medals at the 1994 Winter Olympics.

▼ Dæhlie overtakes a competitor with an earlier start time to win gold in the 10-kilometer cross country.

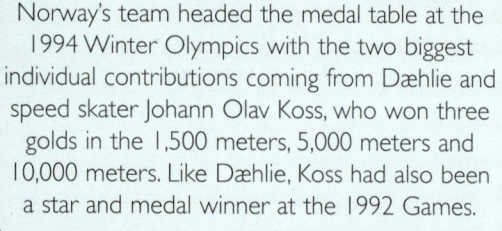

Annemarie Moser-Pröll
Austria, born 1953

Annemarie Moser-Pröll of Austria was one of the finest ever women's downhill and giant slalom skiers. She holds the women's record total of sixty-two wins in World Cup races.

As Annemarie Pröll (until her marriage in 1975), she became the youngest-ever overall World Cup champion in 1971, and dominated the sport for the rest of the 1970s (apart from 1976 when she did not compete).

Moser-Pröll was overall World Cup champion six times (in 1971–75 and in 1979). In her "poor" years of 1977, 1978 and 1980 she was second.

Moser-Pröll won two silver medals in the 1972 Olympics and did not compete in 1976. In 1980 it seemed that she might miss out on the top medals once again, but on the day Moser-Pröll avenged earlier defeats and took the downhill gold.

▲ Annemarie Moser-Pröll (right) and one of her Austrian teammates during the 1974 season.

The Alpine Combined Events
The downhill skiing races are a test of the skiers' speed, while the various types of slalom race put more emphasis on weaving and turning. The overall or Alpine Combined title combines the points achieved in these very different skills—Annemarie Moser-Pröll won it in six World Cups.

◀ Annemarie Moser-Pröll's strongest event was downhill racing in which she was World Cup champion seven times.

Alberto Tomba
Italy, born 1966

Italian winter sports fans had one big favorite in the late 1980s and early 1990s—Alberto Tomba—one of the finest-ever slalom skiers.

Tomba has reserved his top performances for the Olympic Games seasons and 1987–8 was his best year. He was World Cup winner in both the slalom and giant slalom for his performances throughout the season, and he won gold medals in the 1988 Olympics in both events.

The next Olympic year of 1992 was almost as good. Again he won the World Cup in both of his events, but this time he had to settle for a single Olympic gold in the giant slalom. He was back again at the Winter Olympics in 1994, winning a silver medal in the slalom

▲ Tomba on his way to the slalom gold at the 1988 Calgary Olympics.

races to round off a season when he took the overall slalom title.

Because Tomba does not race in the downhill, it is impossible for him to win the Alpine Combined title. However, he has had so many slalom wins that he has three times been second and twice third in the Combined competition.

▼ Tomba prepares for a race in 1993.

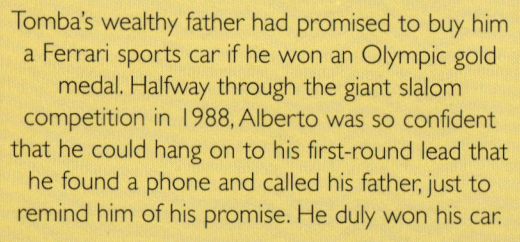

Tomba's wealthy father had promised to buy him a Ferrari sports car if he won an Olympic gold medal. Halfway through the giant slalom competition in 1988, Alberto was so confident that he could hang on to his first-round lead that he found a phone and called his father, just to remind him of his promise. He duly won his car.

Matti Nykänen
Finland, born 1963

Ski jumping is a sport in which the top stars must combine aggression and strength with poise and control. If they manage to achieve this, they will get the best possible lift off from the ski ramp and fly efficiently through the air. Matti Nykänen was simply the best at this difficult combination for most of the 1980s.

Matti Nykänen demonstrated his superiority most convincingly in the Olympic Games. On the 70-meter hill, he won silver in 1984, and gold in 1988.

His jumping on the large 90-meter hill was even better. He took the gold medal in both 1984 and 1988, and was part of the winning Finnish team on the 90-meter hill in 1988 when this was first made a team event.

▼ Matti Nykänen's first round jump in winning the 1988 Olympic 90-meter gold medal was 388 feet 9 inches, the longest ever in an Olympics.

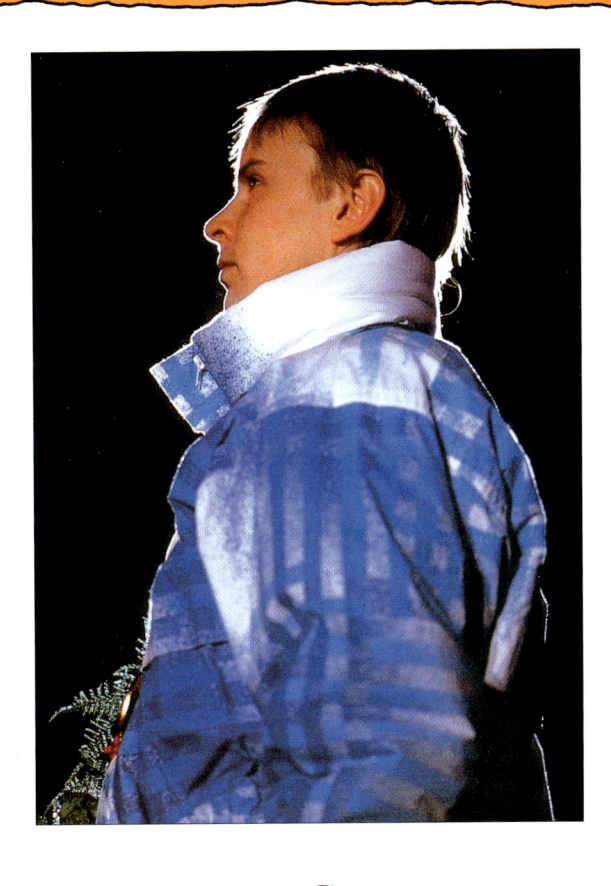

Eddie the Eagle
While Nykänen was winning his gold medals in 1988, a British competitor, Eddie "The Eagle" Edwards, was entertaining the crowds with his bravery, if not with his ski jumping skills. Eddie was last in the competition with less than half of the points scored by the second worst jumper.

Ajax Amsterdam
Netherlands, founded 1900

Ajax of Amsterdam have been one of the best clubs in the Netherlands for many years, but from the 1960s they became one of the best in Europe as well.

Inspired by players such as Johan Cruyff and using the new tactics of "total football," Ajax won successive European Cups in 1971–73.

Another glory period began in 1987 when they won the Cup Winners Cup. In 1992, Ajax became only the second club to win all three European club competitions when they took the EUFA Cup. Perhaps the sweetest success was still to come, however. In 1995 they again won the European Cup, beating AC Milan in the final.

Total Football
The Ajax team and the Dutch national side in the early 1970s based their tactics around what came to be known as "total football." Although players did still specialize in attacking, midfield or defensive play, they were encouraged to take up attacking opportunities whatever position they played on the team.

▼ When Ajax (in dark colors) beat AC Milan 1–0 in the 1995 European Cup Final, it was a long delayed revenge. AC Milan had beaten Ajax 4–1 in Ajax's first ever European final in 1970.

Roberto Baggio
Italy, born 1967

Roberto Baggio came to the 1994 World Cup finals with the hopes of the whole of Italy riding on his goal-scoring abilities. Italy scraped through the group stages of the tournament but, when it came to the knock-out games, Baggio seemed ready to be his team's star.

Baggio scored both the Italian goals to put Nigeria out, scored the winner against Spain in the quarterfinals, and both of Italy's two goals against Bulgaria in the semifinals to gain them a place in the final with Brazil. After all that who could have believed it when Baggio missed the last penalty in the shoot-out to decide the drawn match?

Baggio has played all his club soccer in Italy's famous Serie A league. His first club was Fiorentina and his fans were so disappointed when he left to join Juventus in 1990 that there were riots in the town. Even with Baggio, Juventus found the Italian league title beyond their grasp, but they did win the EUFA Cup in 1993 with Baggio at the top of his form.

That season he was made World and European Player of the Year, but the disappointment of the 1994 World Cup was still to come. Baggio is still one of the game's biggest stars and will have other opportunities to add to his goal-scoring feats.

▲ Baggio playing for Italy in the 1994 World Cup.

Penalty Shoot-outs
The 1994 final was the first time that a World Cup had been won on penalties when the game had been drawn after extra time, although two earlier matches in the 1994 tournament had also gone this way. Three previous World Cup Finals had been won in extra time.

◀ Roberto Baggio in the famous striped colors of Juventus in an Italian league match.

Franz Beckenbauer
West Germany, born 1945

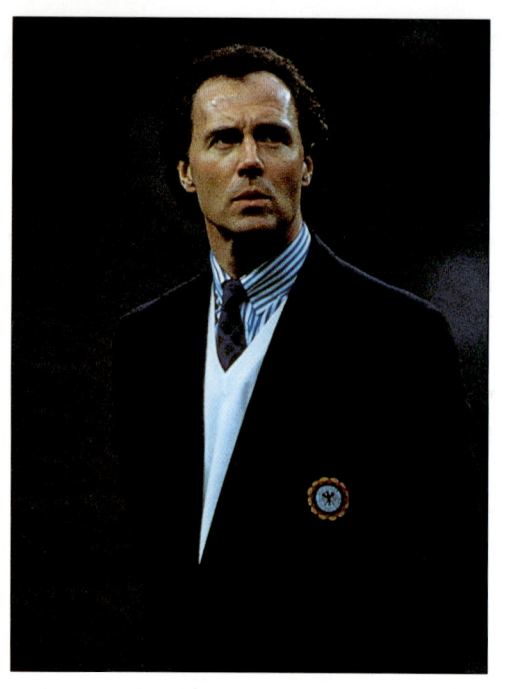

In his playing career, Franz Beckenbauer won a record total of 103 international caps (since beaten) for West Germany, and captained their winning World Cup side in 1974 when they beat tournament favorites Holland in a closely contested final.

In club soccer, he played for most of his career with Bayern Munich, winning numerous trophies in the German football league and leading the club to successive European Cup victories in 1974–6.

Beckenbauer led his teams from the heart of the defense. His marking and tackling were excellent, but he is remembered most for his ability to turn defense into attack with decisive passing or his own forward runs, and powerful long-distance shooting.

Later in his career, in 1977, Beckenbauer joined an American team, the New York Cosmos, where he played an important part in the development of soccer in North America.

After he had retired as a player, Beckenbauer had an equally distinguished career as a coach of the West German national team. He managed them to the runners-up spot in the 1986 World Cup, and went one better in Rome four years later when West Germany beat Argentina 1–0 in the final. Beckenbauer is the only man to have both captained and managed a winning World Cup team.

Fact File
International career: 103 appearances for West Germany
As player: World Cup winners 1974 (as captain), runners-up 1966, semifinals 1970; European Champions 1972
As manager: World Cup winners 1990, runners-up 1986
With Bayern Munich: numerous German trophies; European Cup 1974, 1975, 1976

◀ Franz Beckenbauer in action for West Germany against Brazil in 1973. The next year Beckenbauer led his country to a World Cup triumph.

George Best
Great Britain/Northern Ireland, born 1946

George Best was another of the wayward geniuses who seem to be all too common at the highest levels of international soccer.

Throughout his best years Best played with Manchester United and was an undoubted star in English and European club soccer. He could play as a winger or as a central attacker and used his effortless ball control and pace to tease and bewilder his opponents.

1967 brought the finest moment of his career. United reached the European Cup final against Benfica of Portugal, and an outstanding performance by Best helped them to win 4–1 after extra time.

Later in his career he played less successfully in the U.S. and Scotland as well as for other teams in England.

▼ George Best in the familiar red of Manchester United for whom he played all his finest games.

The Playboy Footballer
George Best was one of the first footballers to live and be treated by fans like a pop star. He dressed in the latest fashions, was seen with beautiful women, and enjoyed going to the top night spots. Unfortunately, this led to his decline as a player, because he also drank too much alcohol and neglected his physical fitness.

Bobby Charlton
Great Britain/England, born 1937

Bobby Charlton was one of the heroes of England's dramatic extra-time win over West Germany in the 1966 World Cup Final, and was selected as European Footballer of the Year in 1966. Charlton made a total of 106 appearances for England (since beaten by two other players) and scored forty-nine goals for his country, which remains the record.

Charlton played for the Manchester United club for almost the whole of his career—in 606 matches he scored 198 goals. Although his powerful shooting and goal-scoring feats are well remembered, Charlton was not an out-and-out striker. His all-round skills made him a brilliant playmaker also.

Since he retired from playing, Charlton has become one of the best-liked and best-known ambassadors of his sport.

▶ Bobby Charlton with the ball in his last game for Manchester United.

▼ A young Charlton shows the power of his shooting.

The Munich Air Disaster
Charlton was one of a group of young players who helped Manchester United to the English championship in 1956 and 1957, and who seemed set to dominate the English game for some years to come. Instead, eight were tragically killed in an air crash when traveling home from a European Cup match in 1958.

Johan Cruyff
Netherlands, born 1947

Johan Cruyff was the leading Dutch soccer player for most of the 1970s. He helped to make the Netherlands one of the most powerful soccer countries in the world.

Cruyff played for Ajax Amsterdam from the start of his career in 1964 until 1973 and later with Barcelona. During his time at Ajax, they won the European Cup three years in succession from 1971 to 1973. Cruyff played forty-eight times for the Dutch national team from 1966, including winning a runners-up medal in the 1974 World Cup.

Cruyff had further success as a coach after his retirement, taking Ajax to the European Cup Winners Cup in 1987, and Barcelona to the Cup Winners Cup in 1989 and the European Cup in 1992.

▼ Cruyff often looked ungainly on the football field, until you saw what he could do with the ball.

> Cruyff got his start at Ajax thanks to his mother. She worked as a cleaner in the club offices and persuaded them that her young son had the sort of talent that the club needed. They took a look at 12-year-old Johan and quickly signed him up for their youth team. The rest, as they say, is history.

Eusébio
Mozambique/Portugal, born 1942

Eusébio was sometimes described as the "European Pelé" which was unfair to his own special footballing skills—the most impressive part of his game was his thunderously powerful shooting.

He was born Eusébio Ferreira da Silva in what was then Portuguese East Africa (now Mozambique) but moved to the Benfica club in Portugal in 1961. At this time he became known by the single name, Eusébio.

Benfica was the best team in Portugal throughout the 1960s and won the European Cup in 1961 and 1962. Eusébio scored two goals in the spectacular 5–3 win in the 1962 final against the Spanish team Real Madrid.

Eusébio played sixty-four games for Portugal and scored forty-one goals. He was top scorer in the 1966 World Cup.

▼▶ Two pictures of Eusébio during the 1963 European Cup final. Eusébio scored, but Benfica finally lost 2–1 to AC Milan.

When Eusébio began playing, the top Portuguese clubs recruited the best players from their country's African colonies. SC Lourenço Marques usually sent players to Sporting Lisbon, but when Eusébio came from them to Portugal in 1961, Benfica persuaded him to join them instead.

Inter Milan
Italy, founded 1908

Milan is soccer-mad and Internazionale, as the side is correctly known, is one of the two teams which divides the city's loyalties. Internazionale was founded after a dispute within AC Milan, when a group of supporters set up their own club in protest at AC Milan's owners.

Internazionale soon became one of Italy's most successful clubs and was one of the pioneers of European club competition in the 1930s. In the 1960s, under coach Helenio Herrera, their defensive *catenaccio* (curtain) formation may not have made for entertaining games, but it was brutally effective.

Internazionale won the European and World Club Championships in 1964 and 1965 and lost in the final in 1967 as their success slipped away. Renewed success came in 1989 with the Italian title, and two UEFA Cup wins in the 1990s.

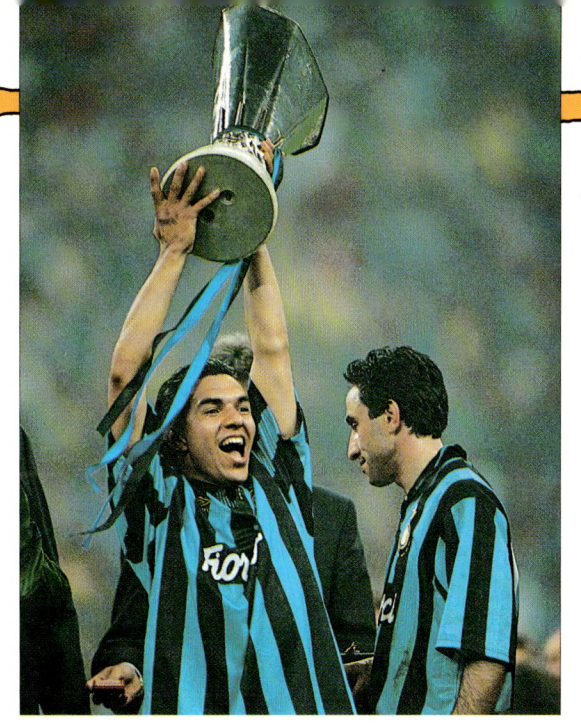

▲ Ruben Sosa hoists the UEFA Cup trophy after Inter Milan's victory in the 1994 final.

Fact File
Club founded: 1908
Italian League champions: thirteen times
Italian Cup winners: three times
European Cup winners: 1964, 1965
UEFA Cup winners: 1991, 1994

Gary Lineker
Great Britain/England, born 1960

Gary Lineker was England's leading goal scorer in the 1980s and one of his country's top marksmen ever. He began his professional career with the modest Leicester City club in 1978, and played with them until 1985 when he joined Everton.

He was English player of the year in 1986, and rounded off a fine season by being overall top scorer in the 1986 World Cup, although England lost in the quarter-finals. Lineker then faced a new challenge with the Spanish club Barcelona, enjoying success when they won the European Cup Winners Cup in 1989.

He returned to England that year to play with Tottenham Hotspur, winning an FA Cup medal with Spurs in 1991 and was made England captain in 1990. He retired with forty-eight goals from his eighty England games, one short of Bobby Charlton's record.

▲ Gary Lineker playing for England (in white) against Scotland (in blue).

▼ Gary Lineker playing for England (in white shirts). against Ireland (in green).

Throughout his playing career, Lineker was one of the fairest ever top players. He was never given a yellow (warning) or red (send off) card for indiscipline by a referee, and this remarkable record was recognized by a special award from soccer's world governing body FIFA.

Manchester United
Great Britain, founded 1878

Manchester United is not England's most successful team (Liverpool has won twice as many championships), but it is the most famous club and has the most fans both in England and around the world.

Their great days began in 1945 when Matt Busby arrived as manager. The achievements of his best team, the "Busby Babes," were cruelly cut short when eight of them were killed in an air crash in 1958. One of the survivors was Bobby Charlton, who was joined by Denis Law and George Best in the next great United side of the 1960s.

Recent years have also been very successful. The best result of all was an historic League and Cup double in 1994 which finished with a 4–0 win over Chelsea in the FA Cup Final.

▼ United players celebrate their League win in 1994.

▲ Cantona scores in the 1994 Cup Final win.

Fact File
English League Champions: 1908, 1911, 1952, 1956, 1957, 1965, 1967, 1993, 1994
FA Cup winners: 1909, 1948, 1963, 1977, 1983, 1985, 1990, 1994
European Cup winners: 1968
European Cup Winners Cup winners: 1991
European Supercup winners: 1991

Diego Maradona
Argentina, born 1960

Diego Maradona was the best soccer player in the world from the late 1970s and throughout most of the 1980s. Despite his marvelous skills, his behavior on and off the field was often unacceptable, and his international career finally ended in disgrace when he was found to have taken drugs to help him to lose weight during the 1994 World Cup.

The first years of his career were spent in his native Argentina, playing mostly for the Argentinos Júniors club. He made his international debut for Argentina at the age of sixteen in 1977. He transferred to Barcelona in Spain in 1982, and moved on from there to Napoli in Italy in 1986, each time for record transfer fees.

Maradona did not play on the Argentina team that won the World Cup in 1978, but was soon a fixture on the side and became its inspiration. His ball control and ability to beat an opponent and make scoring chances out of the slightest opportunity made him a player feared and respected around the world.

He was the mainstay of the Argentina side that won the World Cup in 1986 but, with less able teammates, had to settle for a runners-up spot in 1990.

▲ Maradona wearing Argentina colors in a five-a-side match.

◀ Diego Maradona during his comeback before the 1994 World Cup, when he played for Seville.

Argentina in the World Cup
Argentina ranks fourth in the all-time table of results in the World Cup. The team was second in the first-ever tournament in 1930, won in 1978 and 1986, and gained second place in 1990. Maradona won the award as the tournament's best player in 1986.

Stanley Matthews
Great Britain/England, born 1915

The teams Stanley Matthews played on won only one major trophy, but he is still regarded as one of the greatest players ever to play the game. Matthews was a right-winger who used his brilliant dribbling skills, deceptive swerve and killing acceleration to leave defenders floundering behind him. Once in the open, he delivered inch-perfect crosses to give his attacking teammates perfect scoring opportunities.

Matthews first played for Stoke City in 1932 and England in 1934. He was still on the England team twenty-three years later in 1957, and played his last big match in 1965 when he was over 50 years of age.

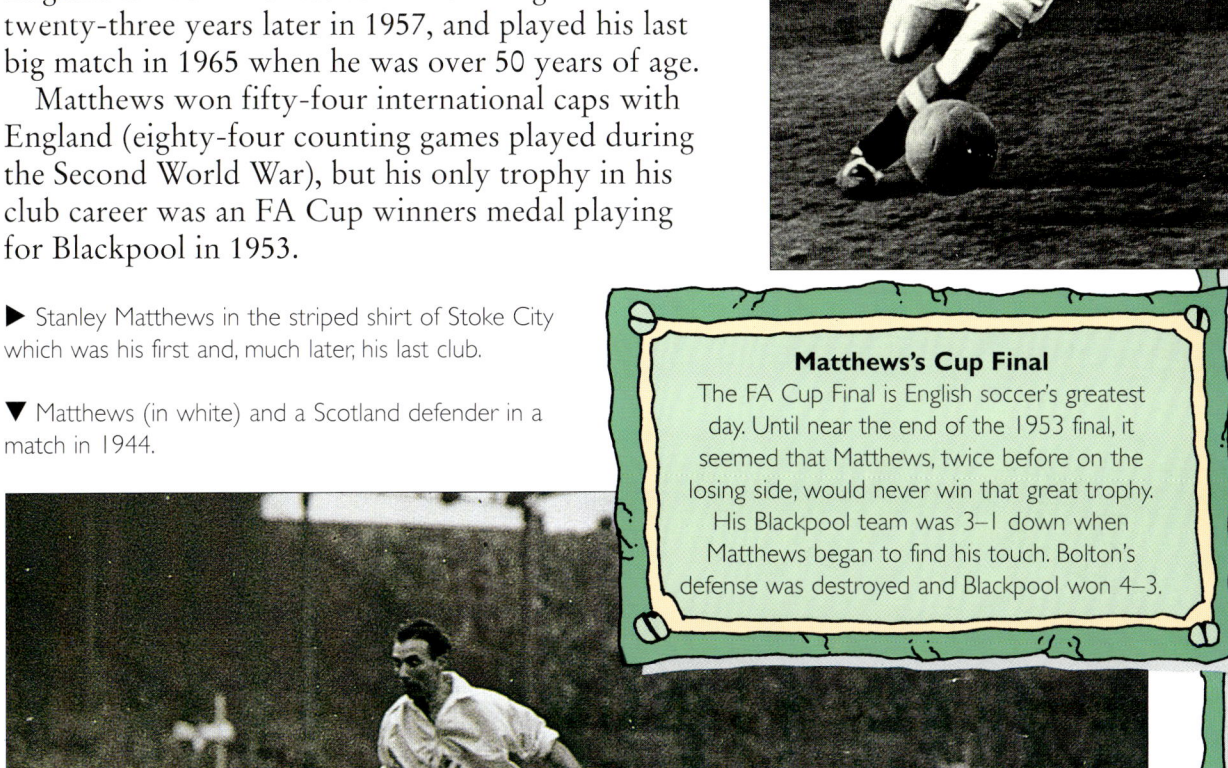

Matthews won fifty-four international caps with England (eighty-four counting games played during the Second World War), but his only trophy in his club career was an FA Cup winners medal playing for Blackpool in 1953.

▶ Stanley Matthews in the striped shirt of Stoke City which was his first and, much later, his last club.

▼ Matthews (in white) and a Scotland defender in a match in 1944.

Matthews's Cup Final
The FA Cup Final is English soccer's greatest day. Until near the end of the 1953 final, it seemed that Matthews, twice before on the losing side, would never win that great trophy. His Blackpool team was 3–1 down when Matthews began to find his touch. Bolton's defense was destroyed and Blackpool won 4–3.

Pelé
Brazil, born 1940

Pelé was born Edson Arantes do Nascimento, but under the name by which he is usually known he became the world's best-ever soccer player.

In 1957, aged only seventeen, Pelé scored a goal in the first game he played for Brazil, and in 1958 he was the star of the Brazilian team that won the World Cup. He triumphed again in 1970 on the magnificent Brazil team that won the World Cup, scoring the first goal in the 4–1 win over Italy in the final.

In club soccer, he played for most of his career with Santos, helping them to two South American club championships in the Copa Libertadores in 1962 and 1963, plus many other domestic Brazilian trophies. He played out the final years of his career with the New York Cosmos, helping to increase the popularity of soccer in the U.S.

▲ Pelé with his foot beside the ball ready to take a free kick in his last Brazil international in 1971.

▼ Pelé early in his international career.

Pelé published his life story under the title *My Life and the Beautiful Game*. Most people who saw him remember how he made soccer just that, blending his sparkling skills with his delight in attacking tactics. Many people think that the Brazilian team starring Pelé in 1970 was the finest ever.

Ferenc Puskas
Hungary/Spain, born 1927

Even his own fans said that Ferenc Puskas was unfit and overweight, and that his right foot was only good for standing on, but that was not important since he could do anything he wanted with his left.

Puskas first played for the Kispest club in his native Hungary from 1943, staying with them when they became Honved in 1948. Through the 1950s, Puskas played 84 games for Hungary and scored 83 goals. Unfortunately, he had to settle for a second place medal in the 1954 World Cup.

In 1958, Puskas joined Real Madrid. The Spanish team was the best club side in the world at the time, and Puskas's partnership in attack with the Argentinian Alfredo di Stefano took them to still more honors. They won the European Cup in 1959 and 1960 and the Spanish championship each year between 1961 and 1965.

▶ Puskas (dark shirt) and a Swedish player tussle for the ball in a 1955 game when Puskas was playing for Hungary.

▼ Puskas warms up before a match for Spain against England in 1963.

Puskas's Greatest Game
The European Cup Final in 1960 saw Puskas at his best. His partner Alfredo di Stefano scored three goals, but Puskas scored four as Real Madrid overwhelmed the German team Eintracht Frankfurt 7–3 in what many fans say was the best game they have ever seen.

Michel Platini
France, born 1955

Michel Platini was France's best-ever soccer player, and is the only man ever to win the European Player of the Year award three times in a row (1983–5).

Platini was a gifted midfield organizer. His passing skills opened up opposition defenses, and he scored many important goals from free kicks and penalties as well as in open play.

Platini came to the fore with the French club Nancy, which he joined in 1972. He won a place on the French national team in 1976, and eventually won seventy-two caps. He played successfully from 1979 to 1982 with St Etienne in France and from 1982 to 1987 with Juventus in Italy. After he retired in 1987, Platini became coach of the French national team, but was replaced in 1992 after disappointing results.

▲ Platini celebrates a goal for France, World Cup 1986.

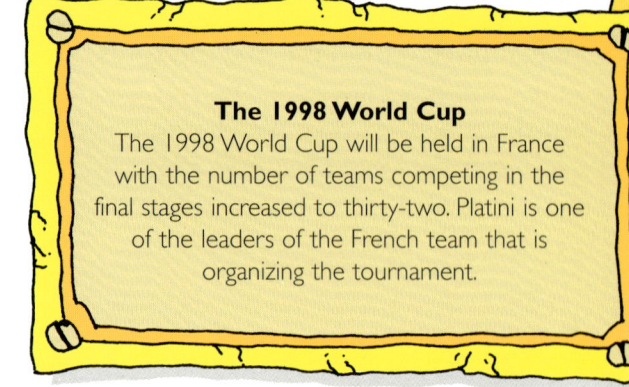

The 1998 World Cup
The 1998 World Cup will be held in France with the number of teams competing in the final stages increased to thirty-two. Platini is one of the leaders of the French team that is organizing the tournament.

▼ Platini sets up a shooting opportunity for Juventus.

Marco van Basten
Netherlands, born 1964

Marco van Basten was one of the finest players in the seemingly endless stream of great soccer stars that the Netherlands has produced since the 1960s.

Van Basten's club soccer career began with the famous Ajax Amsterdam club (see page 66). His goal-scoring ability helped Ajax to six major trophies in Dutch football and the Cup Winners Cup in 1987.

Later in 1987, van Basten was transferred to AC Milan of Italy. Van Basten was one of the driving forces of the success that followed. Milan won the Italian championship in 1988 and 1993, and took the European Cup in 1989 (with two goals in the final from van Basten) and 1990. He retired in the summer of 1995.

▲ Marco van Basten in Italian league action with AC Milan. Van Basten was European player of the year in 1988, 1989 and 1992.

▼ Van Basten (in orange) was a star with the Dutch national team. He scored in the final when Holland won the European Championship in 1988.

FIFA World Footballer of the Year
This award was officially made for the first time in 1991 and amazingly the first three winners all played in Italy. Lothar Matthäus of Inter Milan and Germany won in 1991, Marco van Basten of AC Milan and the Netherlands in 1992, and Roberto Baggio of Juventus and Italy in 1993.

Taiho
Japan, born 1940

Wrestlers in Japan's national sport of sumo are given special names. Taiho means "Big Bird" in Japanese, and the man who used this name is regarded as the greatest-ever sumo wrestler. His original family name was Koki Naya.

Taiho won thirty-two of the most important tournaments, the Emperor's Cup, held six times each year, more than twice as many as any other sumo wrestler ever. In eight of these wins, his dominance was so complete that he did not lose a single one of the fifteen bouts that each wrestler must fight in the tournament. Taiho had his final victory in 1971, after which he retired.

Foreigners in Japan's national sport
In recent years, a number of non-Japanese people, mostly from Pacific islands, have become well-known sumo wrestlers, and there was considerable debate in Japan as to whether they should qualify for the highest ranking titles in the sport.

▲ Taiho with the Emperor's Cup in 1961 after one of his first top wins. He was promoted to *Yokozuna* or "Grand Champion" in the official rankings for this success. Taiho was the youngest-ever *Yokozuna*.

▼ Taiho (center) and other wrestlers perform the opening ceremonies before a tournament.

Konishiki
Samoa/U.S., born 1963

Konishiki is one of a now-growing number of non-Japanese who have carved out a great career in Japan's national sport of sumo wrestling. Konishiki was born in Hawaii and has Samoan ancestors. His original name was Salevaa Fuali Atisanoe. As well as his official wrestling name, he is also known as "The Dumptruck" because of his huge size.

> Konishiki is 6 feet 2 inches tall and at his top weight of 589 lb was the heaviest sumo wrestler ever. Sumo wrestlers eat a special high protein stew called *chunkonabe* to build up their huge weight and strength. Some wrestlers even open restaurants specializing in this dish after they retire from the ring.

▲ Konishiki preparing to hoist an opponent out of the ring at the Grand Sumo tournament in Honolulu.

▼ Konishiki (right) and Kirishima perform a *shiko* (prematch ritual) before a ritual tournament in Tokyo.

He shocked the sumo world in 1984 in his second tournament in the top division. He beat the two reigning *Yokozuna* (grand champions) and nearly won the tournament—an astonishing feat for a rookie and a foreigner at that.

Injuries slowed his progress and he did not reach the second to top rank of *Ozeki* (champion) until 1987. More knee problems followed and seemed to cut down his speed in the ring. But in 1989 through to the start of 1992, he was at his best. He won three major tournaments and was placed high in others. All Japan wondered if he would be the first-ever foreigner to make the top grade of *Yokozuna.* But it was not to be and he slipped down the rankings once more.

Swimming

Kornelia Ender
East Germany, born 1958

Kornelia Ender was one of the biggest stars of swimming during the 1970s. Ender won numerous big championships and set world records in her events a total of twenty-three times.

She competed at the 1972 Olympics when she was still only 13 years old for the then German Democratic Republic. But even at that young age she was a force to be reckoned with and won three silver medals. She went on to set her first world record, in the 100-meters freestyle, in 1973 when she was 14 years old. She improved on that record nine more times, eventually setting a personal best of 55.65 seconds.

Ender's biggest year was 1976 when she became the first woman ever to win four gold medals at one Olympic Games. Her great triumphs came in the 100-meters and 200-meters freestyle, the 100-meters butterfly, and the 400-meters medley relay. To finish off a great competition, she also recorded a silver in the 400-meters freestyle relay.

◀ Kornelia Ender waves from the victory stand after winning her fourth gold medal (in the women's 200-meters freestyle) at the Montreal Olympics in 1976.

▼ Kornelia Ender swimming in a heat of the women's 100-meters butterfly at Montreal.

Fact File
Olympic success: 4 gold medals, 4 silvers
World Championship successes: 8 gold medals, 2 silvers (1973 & 1975)
European Championships: 4 gold medals
23 world records—most ever by a woman in currently recognized events

Michael Gross
West Germany, born 1964

Michael Gross was one of the most successful and versatile swimmers competing during the 1980s.

By the 1982 world championships, Gross had reached the peak of his form, and won gold medals in both the 200 meters butterfly and freestyle. In the 1984 Olympics, he confirmed his status with wins in the 200 meters freestyle and 100 meters butterfly, both achieved in world-record times.

Gross successfully defended his two world championship titles in 1986, and in the 1988 Olympics he won the 200 meters butterfly. He did this in the best possible style, taking the gold in a new Olympic record time.

Gross was a tall man at 6 feet 8 inches, but his most astonishing physical feature was the huge length of his arms which were 6 feet 11 inches from fingertip to fingertip. The bird with the world's biggest wingspan is the albatross, so Gross was nicknamed "The Albatross."

▲ Michael Gross with one of the three European Championship gold medals he won in 1983. He won 13 golds in all in various European Championships.

▼ The Albatross spreads his "wings" and powers ahead in another butterfly race.

Mark Spitz
U.S., born 1950

California-born Mark Spitz was the outstanding athlete of the 1972 Olympic Games and one of America's greatest-ever sporting stars.

Spitz had gone to the 1968 Mexico Olympics strongly favored in several of the swimming events, but was very upset to win only one silver and one bronze medal in individual races, although he did swim on two gold-medal-winning U.S. relay teams.

This disappointment gave him all the motivation he needed in 1972 to dominate a series of swimming races as no other man has ever done. Mark Spitz won an amazing seven gold medals at the Munich Olympics. Even more astonishingly, all of these races were won in world record times. The races were the 100-meters and 200-meters freestyle and butterfly individual events, plus the relays of 4 x 100-meters and 4 x 200-meters freestyle, and the 4 x 100-meters medley.

Spitz's career of record-breaking performances included twenty-six occasions when he set or improved individual world records and another six when he was part of record-breaking teams. These records included all his gold medal events and in addition the 400-meters freestyle. Mark Spitz is America's greatest swimmer to date.

▼ Mark Spitz winning the men's 200-meter butterfly at the Munich Olympic Games in 1972.

> Almost all swimmers retire from competition when they are quite young. Mark Spitz tried to prove that this was a mistake when he made a comeback in 1991. He wanted to win a place on the 1992 U.S. Olympic team. But aged 41, he proved to be too old to match the top racers from the younger generation.

Arthur Ashe
U.S., 1943–93

Arthur Ashe was an African-American and is remembered for succeeding in a sport that before his time had been an almost completely white game.

Ashe had a successful sporting career at the University of California in Los Angeles, during which he was three times named as All-American and won the NCAA singles title in 1965.

After graduating, he served in the U.S. Army and so at first did not play full-time tennis. In 1968, however, he won the U.S. Open. He would later go on to win the Australian Open in 1970 and, his finest triumph of all, Wimbledon in 1975. In the Wimbledon final he beat the world number one and defending champion, Jimmy Connors.

▼ Arthur Ashe stretches for a backhand stroke during his Wimbledon final in 1975.

▲ Arthur Ashe celebrating his 1975 Wimbledon success with the championship trophy.

> Throughout his life, Ashe was a notable campaigner against racism. As a boy he had been forbidden from playing in school tournaments in Virginia where he was born. Later he worked to improve civil rights throughout the U.S., and against Apartheid in South Africa. In the final years of his life, he also established a foundation to advance AIDS research.

Ashe was proud of his record in U.S. Davis Cup teams. He won twenty-seven of his thirty-two Davis Cup singles and, after he stopped playing, was non-playing captain of the winning U.S. team in 1981 and 1982. Ashe had to stop playing following a heart attack in 1979, and died in 1993 of an AIDS-related illness because he had been infected with HIV by a contaminated blood transfusion during heart surgery.

Björn Borg
Sweden, born 1956

Björn Borg was the man to beat at Wimbledon in the second half of the 1970s, but nobody did. The Swede holds the amazing record of winning the Wimbledon singles title five years in succession from 1976 to 1980.

The final in 1980 in which Borg beat one of his great rivals, the American John McEnroe, is said to have been one of the greatest matches of all time. They played five sets of superlative tennis with a nail-biting tie-break in the fourth set, which McEnroe won, only for Borg to make an astonishing comeback and take the final set 8–6.

Borg relied less on the serve and volley tactics used by most of the top

▼ ▶ Two pictures of Björn Borg during his 1979 Wimbledon singles success. Borg was one of the last top players to use the traditional wooden racket.

Borg led the Swedish team to his country's first-ever win in the Davis Cup in 1975, and he won thirty-seven out of the forty singles matches that he played in the Cup competitions.
His success also inspired later Swedish players to win the competition three times out of seven appearances in the final in the 1980s.

men, and instead cultivated fierce ground strokes, including a powerful two-handed backhand. His strongest assets, however, were probably his total concentration and determination.

As well as his five Wimbledon titles, Borg also won the French Open a record six times, but never succeeded in the Australian Open or the U.S. Open, where he lost in the final four times. He retired in 1983 and made an unsuccessful comeback in the early 1990s.

Jimmy Connors
U.S., born 1952

Jimmy Connors first made his mark on the world of tennis when he won the U.S. Collegiate championship in 1971. He then joined the professional circuit and quickly became one of its stars.

Like his great rival for much of the 1970s, the Swede Björn Borg, Connors did not rely on the traditional serve and volley tactics of the other stars of men's tennis. His ground strokes and return of service were his best shots, and he backed them up with all-out effort and a determination never to lose.

Connors was the world number one from 1974 to 1978, and won five of his total of eight top singles titles in these years. His best year was 1974 when he

▼ Jimmy Connors puts all his power into this two-handed backhand stroke during a match in the 1985 Wimbledon championships.

Fact File
World number one: 1974–8
Total weeks as number one: 268 (1974–83)
Wimbledon Champion: 1974, 1982
U.S. Open Champion: 1975, 1976, 1982, 1983
Tournament wins: 109 singles titles
Career earnings: $8,471,435

won the Australian, U.S. and Wimbledon championships, and might have won the French title as well if he had not been stopped from playing in it because of an off-court dispute.

Connors had another period of good fortune in 1982–3, winning Wimbledon in 1982 and the U.S. Open at Forest Hills in both of those years. He went on to play at the top level until 1992, often beating the younger players who had taken over as the best in the game.

Margaret Court
Australia, born 1942

By almost every measurement, Margaret Court was the best tennis player ever, man or woman. She was brought up in a small town in New South Wales in Australia, and as a youngster she played much of her tennis against men because they were the only available opponents who could give her a good game. She adopted the serve and volley style of play, and added to it speed around the court and natural athletic ability.

Court is one of only three women and two men to have won a "Grand Slam" of the top singles tournaments. She completed this feat in 1970, and won three out of the four major championships in an additional four years. She was also a top doubles player.

▼ Margaret Court during the Wimbledon leg of her great 1970 "Grand Slam" of the top singles titles.

▲ The young Margaret Smith in action in 1963.

Her win at Wimbledon in 1970 was one of her finest. Although she was hampered by an ankle injury and her opponent was the formidable Billie Jean King, Court won a marathon two-set victory 14–12, 11–9 (in those days, tie-breaks were not used).

Court competed at the top level from 1959 to 1977 and was known by her maiden name, Margaret Smith, until her marriage in 1967.

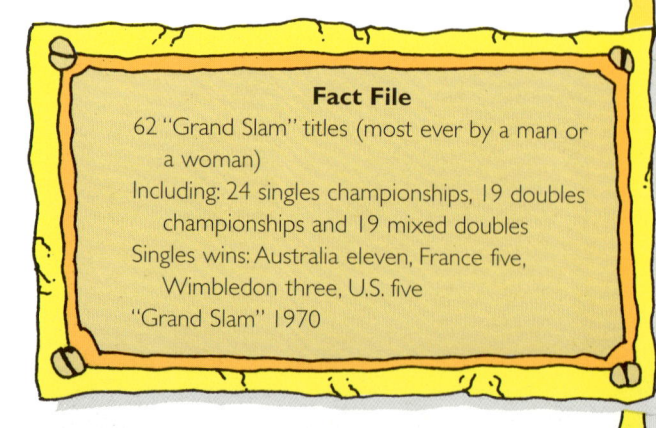

Fact File
62 "Grand Slam" titles (most ever by a man or a woman)
Including: 24 singles championships, 19 doubles championships and 19 mixed doubles
Singles wins: Australia eleven, France five, Wimbledon three, U.S. five
"Grand Slam" 1970

Steffi Graf
Germany, born 1969

Steffi Graf is one of only three women ever to have won a "Grand Slam" of tennis's top four singles tournaments, and, even more sensationally, she did it in 1988 when she was aged only nineteen.

Steffi first began to get noticed in the summer of 1986, when she turned sixteen, and notched up wins over the two best players in the world, Chris Evert and Martina Navratilova. In 1987 she had her first big tournament success when she took the French Open singles title, beating Navratilova in the final.

Steffi is a strong and athletic player. Her backhand may sometimes be a little weak, but she makes up for it with her powerful and accurate forehand, working

▼ An unusual overhead shot of Steffi Graf serving during the 1994 U.S. Open in which she lost in the final to Arantxa Sanchez Vicario.

▲ Steffi Graf serves during the first round of the 1994 Wimbledon tournament.

> In the four wins that made up her 1988 "Grand Slam," Steffi showed her superiority over her top opponents. Chris Evert was beaten in Australia, Natalia Zvereva in France, Martina Navratilova at Wimbledon and Gabriela Sabatini at the U.S. championships. Then Steffi went to Seoul and won the Olympics as well.

opponents all round the court before passing them with a winning shot.

Women's tennis has seen many young stars come forward in recent years, just like Steffi, only for them to fade away after a brief period at the top. Steffi has proved to be different, winning at least one "Grand Slam" singles title in every year since her great triumphs of 1988.

Billie Jean King
U.S., born 1943

Billie Jean King was a very courageous and attacking American player with a powerful serve and volley at the heart of her game—qualities that made her the world's number one from 1966 to 1974.

Her most successful championship was Wimbledon. She won the singles six times and added ten wins in the doubles and four in the mixed doubles for a total of twenty championships, the best by any player, man or woman. She won all three Wimbledon titles in 1967 and 1973.

King won other major tournaments, too. She won the singles at the U.S. Open four times, and added one win each at the French and Australian championships. She never managed the

▼ Billie Jean King raises the Wimbledon ladies singles trophy high in delight after her win in the tournament in 1975.

The Battle of the Sexes
Billie Jean King won a famous match in 1973 against Bobbie Riggs. Riggs had been a top male player some years before and had begun challenging many of the best women players in exhibition matches.
He could not keep up with King, however, and she beat him in three straight sets.

elusive "Grand Slam" of all four titles in a single year, but in 1972 she won three of them, losing out only in Australia.

Off the court, she worked hard for women's tennis. She was one of the leaders of the women's players' organizations, helping to improve the running of the game and bringing more prize money into it for women. King's maiden name was Billie Jean Moffitt, but she used her married name for most of her tennis career.

Rod Laver
Australia, born 1938

Rod Laver is possibly tennis's greatest ever player. The best proof of that is that he is the only player ever to win tennis's "Grand Slam" of the four top tournaments not once but twice.

to that triumph and the wins in his "Grand Slam" years, Laver won the men's singles at Wimbledon in 1961 and the Australian championship in 1960. Laver was also a superb doubles player. As a member of Australia's Davis Cup team, Laver won all his doubles matches. Australia won the Davis Cup five times when Laver was on the team.

Laver was not a very big or a very strong man. But any opponent who thought he might be easy to beat soon found the ball spinning out of his reach from one of Laver's favorite topspin backhand winners.

◀ Laver shows off the trophy after winning the U.S. National Men's singles title in 1962.

▼ Rod Laver in fine form in the opening men's singles match at Wimbledon in 1969.

If Rod Laver was not the best ever tennis player, then he was certainly the best ever lefthander. There are far more lefthanders among top tennis players than in the ordinary population. So if you are lefthanded and looking for a suitable sport, then perhaps tennis is the game to try.

Laver's two best years were 1962 and 1969. In 1962 Laver also won another six big tournaments in addition to the top four. After that he turned professional and for five years he could not contest the "Grand Slam" titles. Who knows how many more he might have won in those years.

In 1968, when professionals were allowed back into the top tournaments, Laver won at Wimbledon. In addition

Martina Navratilova
Czechoslovakia/U.S., born 1956

Martina Navratilova was the dominant figure in women's tennis for most of the 1980s. She was born and raised in what was then Czechoslovakia and had her first tennis successes as a Czech, reaching the Wimbledon and Australian finals in 1975. Later that year she went to live in the U.S., eventually becoming a U.S. citizen in 1981.

Navratilova was a tall and powerful left-hander who brought new standards of fitness to the women's game. She won eighteen major championship singles titles, including a record nine at Wimbledon.

Her last appearance in the singles at Wimbledon was in 1994, when tennis fans everywhere hoped she might win a record tenth title, but she lost in the final to Conchita Martinez of Spain.

▲ Martina Navratilova at the French championships in 1986. She only won the French title once, in 1984.

The Federation Cup
The Federation Cup is the top team competition in international women's tennis. Navratilova holds the unique distinction of being on the winning side in the Federation Cup for two different countries. She was a member of the Czech team that won in 1975, and of the U.S. teams of 1982, 1986, and 1989.

▼ Navratilova at Wimbledon in 1990 when she won the last of her nine singles titles.

Pete Sampras
U.S., born 1971

In 1995 Pete Sampras was nothing less than the best tennis player in the world. He first reached the number one position in the world rankings in 1993, and has stayed there virtually continuously ever since.

Sampras turned professional in 1988 and started a steady progression to the top. By 1993, he was contesting the top place with the U.S. player Jim Courier, and wins at Wimbledon and in the U.S. Open saw Sampras edge ahead.

Sampras's first major win was in the U.S. Open in 1990, just a few days after his nineteenth birthday. That made him the youngest ever winner of this "Grand Slam" title.

▼ Pete Sampras seems to be all concentration and poise in this picture taken during the 1994 U.S. Open, but he lost surprisingly in the fourth round.

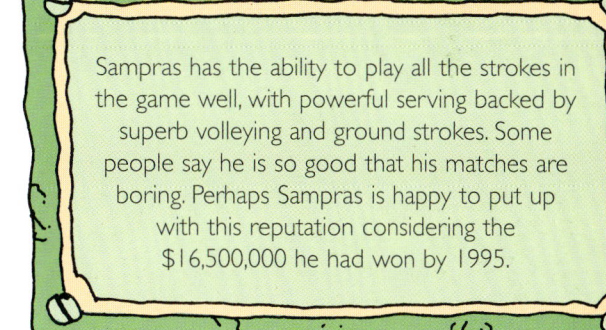

Sampras has the ability to play all the strokes in the game well, with powerful serving backed by superb volleying and ground strokes. Some people say he is so good that his matches are boring. Perhaps Sampras is happy to put up with this reputation considering the $16,500,000 he had won by 1995.

In 1994 he achieved ten wins, including the Australian and Wimbledon titles. Sampras is at his best on the lightning-quick grass courts, but in 1994 his tournament successes were achieved on all four of the types of court used by the top players. In 1995, Sampras added a third successive Wimbledon title, which ranks him among the best in the history of the tournament.

TRIATHLON

Mark Allen
U.S., born 1958

All champion sportsmen and women have to put in many hours of training to achieve success in their various events, but possibly the most difficult of all events is the triathlon. Triathletes must complete three long races one after another in a single day: first a swim, then a cycle ride and finally a long run to complete the competition.

The distances for these various sections vary between competitions, but for the most famous event of all, the Hawaii Ironman Championships, they are a 2-mile swim, followed by a 110-mile cycle ride and then finally a full marathon run of 26.22 miles. For many competitors it is enough simply to finish the course!

▼ The number one on the runner's chest says it all. This is Mark Allen in 1991 in the middle of his sequence of Hawaii Ironman wins.

Women in the Hawaii Triathlon
South Africa's Paula Newby-Fraser has won the women's event in Hawaii seven times. Her record for the course is 8 hours 55 minutes 28 seconds set in 1992, a time which would have been good enough to win the men's race in each year from 1978 to 1983.

The Hawaii race starts at 7:00 a.m. and the course is kept open to midnight to give the slower finishers a chance just to complete the race. The record time is an astonishing 8 hours 7 minutes 45 seconds. That record was set by one of triathlon's finest ever exponents, Mark Allen, when he won the race for the fifth year in succession in 1993.

Allen was also the first-ever men's triathlon world champion (over a shorter course than in Hawaii) when that event was first held in 1989.

Roger Bannister
Great Britain, born 1929

Roger Bannister is famous for an achievement on a single day, in an event that is not even contested very regularly in the modern world. The day was May 6, 1954, and the location was the Oxford University athletics field at Iffley Road in Oxford, England.

In athletics, targets in achievement are continually being set which are finally reached and surpassed. After World War II (1939–45), one target was thought to be impossible—to run a mile in under four minutes. But as the 1950s began, it seemed that this was in sight.

▲ Roger Bannister about to cross the finish line.

On the big day Bannister ran a great race, but had he broken the record? The crowd held their breaths for the announcement of the winning time, but as soon as the announcer said "three minutes...." they did not need to let him finish for they knew already that the record had been achieved.

▼ An exhausted Roger Bannister waits for that special announcement.

Bannister and Landy
Bannister's great rival was an Australian, John Landy. Later in 1954 they ran in the first-ever mile race in which two men both beat four minutes. The current world mile record is 3 minutes 44.39 seconds, and was set by Noureddine Morceli of Algeria (see page 104) in 1993.

Abebe Bikila
Ethiopia, 1932–73

Abebe Bikila came to the 1960 Olympic Games in Rome having run in only two marathons (a distance of 26 miles 385 yards) in his native Ethiopia. He was a soldier and had only begun running competitively after he joined the Ethiopian army when he was already grown up.

In Rome he surprised all the experts by not only winning the marathon, but by doing so in what was then the world record-breaking time of 2 hours 15 minutes 16.2 seconds.

The next Olympic Games were at Tokyo in 1964, and Bikila came back to defend his marathon title. He became the only man to do this successfully, coming home in front in a time of 2 hours 12 minutes 11.2 seconds, which was again the best ever recorded to that date.

▼ ▶ Abebe Bikila during his two Olympic marathon wins. In Rome in 1960 he ran barefoot (above). In Tokyo in 1964, he wore shoes (below).

What was the difference between Bikila's two Olympic marathon wins? For the second one in 1964, he wore shoes! Remarkably his first Olympic success in 1960, in this longest and most punishing of races, was achieved barefoot.

Fanny Blankers-Koen
Netherlands, born 1918

Fanny Blankers-Koen is best remembered for her performance at the 1948 Olympic Games, held in London. She was the world record holder in both the high and long jumps, but did not even compete in these events. Instead, she devoted herself to the track and still ended up with four gold medals from one Olympics, a record that has not been beaten by any other woman in the history of track and field.

Her gold medal performances were achieved in the 100 meters, 200 meters, 80-meters hurdles and the 4 by 100-meters relay. She was even more versatile than this record suggests. During her career, she held world records in eight different events, including all those already mentioned, the 100-yard sprint and the five-event competition, the pentathlon.

Four-time Gold Medal Winners
Only three other track and field athletes have equaled Blankers-Koen's feat of winning four Olympic gold medals, but none won all four at one Olympic Games. They are Betty Cuthbert of Australia (1956 and 1964), Barbel Eckert Wöckel of East Germany (1976 and 1980), and Evelyn Ashford of the U.S. (1984 and 1992).

▲ Fanny Blankers-Koen crosses the finishing line to win the 200 meters at the 1948 Olympics.

▼ Blankers-Koen (nearest the camera) early in her winning 80-meters hurdles race in 1948.

Sergei Bubka
USSR/Ukraine, born 1963

Most top sports stars have a number of close challengers in their events, but occasionally a sport has a single superstar who is so far ahead of all the rest as to be just about unbeatable. Sergei Bubka is one of these rare people.

Bubka surprised everyone when he won the pole vault in the 1983 World Championships. Since this, his first major win, the only real surprise in a pole vault competition was in the 1992 Olympics when he had three failures at his opening heights and was out of the competition. Otherwise he has been supreme.

His first world record came outdoors in 1983, and he has improved his outdoor or indoor mark at least once every year since then. His current indoor and outdoor world records are both a massive 12 inches higher than when he began competing.

▼ Pole vaulters must achieve a special combination of speed in their run up and strength and technique to control the pole and the jump. Sergei Bubka is the best there has ever been.

Bubka's World Records
Bubka has set more world records in a single event than anyone else, but people wonder how often he has been trying his hardest. Bonuses are often given to athletes for new world records and some fans suggest that Bubka has deliberately beaten his own records a little bit at a time to keep earning this extra money.

Jackie Joyner-Kersee
U.S., born 1962

Jackie Joyner-Kersee is one of the greatest ever all-round track and field athletes. Her special skill is the heptathlon, in which points are scored in seven events, over two days of competition. The seven events are: 100 meters, high jump, shot putt, 200 meters, long jump, javelin, and 800 meters.

Joyner-Kersee has simply been the best in the world at this complicated range of skills since the mid-1980s. She won the Olympic gold medal in 1988 with a score of 7,291 points, which is still the world record. She won the Olympic heptathlon again in 1992 and was also world champion in 1987 and 1993.

Joyner-Kersee has also been a formidable competitor in individual events. In the long jump she won Olympic gold in 1988 and the world championship in 1987, 1991 and 1993.

▼ Joyner-Kersee during the javelin section of the 1987 heptathlon World Championship, her first world championship win.

Joyner-Kersee's brother, Al Joyner, won the gold medal in the triple jump in the 1984 Olympics. His wife, Florence Griffith-Joyner (known as Flo-Jo), did even better. She won gold medals in the 100 meters, 200 meters and sprint relay at the 1988 Olympics, as well as a silver medal in the 4 by 400-meters relay.

Marita Koch
East Germany, born 1957

Marita Koch was probably the world's best ever woman sprinter. The 400 meters was her finest event, but she was almost as good at the 200 meters and 100 meters. She retired from competition in 1986, and the world record she set at 400 meters in 1985—47.60 seconds—has not even been threatened since then.

Koch was more than just good at setting records. She could also produce her best performances in the top competitions. From 1978 until she retired in 1986, she was beaten only twice in the 400 meters, and altogether won 17 gold medals at her various distances. She was Olympic 400 meters champion in 1980.

When the World Championships were started in 1983, she won the 200 meters, along with a silver medal in the 100 meters.

▼ Marita Koch (in blue) races in 1977 against one of her great rivals, Irina Szewinska of Poland. Szewinska won this race in a world record time, but it was the last time Marita Koch lost a 400m race for four years.

Drugs in Athletics
Koch competed for the former communist country of East Germany. There are many stories of how the East Germans made their athletes take illegal drugs. Koch was never found to have taken drugs, but some people believe that all the records set by East Germans in those years have been put in doubt.

Carl Lewis
U.S., born 1961

Carl Lewis was one of the finest ever long jumpers and sprinters. His nine gold medals put him far ahead of any modern competitor in the Olympic medal table, and he has also won eight World Championship golds as well.

Lewis's best championship was the 1984 Olympics when he won the gold in all four of his events (long jump, 100 and 200 meters and 4 by 100-meters relay).

In the 100 meters, Lewis set the world record twice and his best time of 9.86 seconds has only been improved by one-hundredth of a second. That was by Leroy Burrell of the U.S. in 1994.

In the 1988 Olympics 100 meters, Canadian runner Ben Johnson crossed the line first in the incredible time of 9.79 seconds, well ahead of Lewis who was in second place. Afterward, Johnson was discovered to have cheated by taking illegal performance-enhancing drugs, and his medal and records were awarded to Lewis.

▲ Lewis was unbeaten in long jump competitions from 1981 to 1991, including here at the 1988 Olympics in Seoul where he took the gold medal.

▼ Carl Lewis (left) celebrates his win in the 1984 Olympic Games 100 meters in front of his home fans in Los Angeles.

Noureddine Morceli
Algeria, born 1970

Noureddine Morceli is the greatest middle-distance track athlete in the world today. He confirmed his supremacy with a great gold-medal-winning performance in the 1,500 meters at the Olympic Games in Atlanta in 1996. He currently holds four outdoor and two indoor world records at various distances.

Morceli first became known to the world of track athletics in 1990 when he won the athletics Grand Prix series. In 1991 he was even better. He won every race at 1,500 meters or one mile that he entered. These victories included World Championships both outdoors and indoors. He also set a world indoor record for 1,500 meters that year which still stands today.

The year 1992 was disappointing for him because he lost several races and finished well out of the medals in the Olympics. But since then he has reeled off race win after race win and has set and then reduced world records at 1,500 meters and one mile. His triumph in Atlanta confirmed that he is truly one of the all-time greats.

Morceli's World Records
1,500 meters, set July 1995: 3 mins 27.37 secs
1 mile, set Sept 1993: 3 mins 44.39 secs
1,500 meters (indoor), set 1991: 3 mins 34.16 secs
Other records held: 2,000 meters, 3,000 meters
1,000 meters indoors

▶ Morceli winning the Wanamaker mile at Madison Square Garden, New York, in 1993.

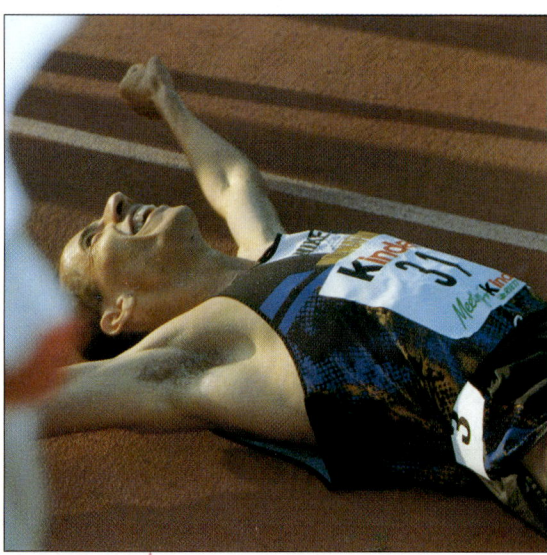

Paavo Nurmi
Finland, 1897–1973

Paavo Nurmi was probably the biggest star of track athletics in the 1920s. He was known as the "Flying Finn." His twelve Olympic medals top the all-time list at track and field and will probably never be broken.

Nurmi's success was based on his tough training schedule, far tougher than most athletes of his time put themselves through. His drive and determination helped him achieve an amazing versatility. He won top-class races at every distance from 800 meters to 20,000 meters.

Nurmi won his nine Olympic gold medals at three different Olympic Games in 1920, 1924, and 1928.

◀ Paavo Nurmi winning the 5,000 meters at the 1924 Olympic Games in Paris, France.

Fact File
1920 Olympics: 10,000m gold medal, cross-country team and individual golds, 5,000m silver
1924 Olympics: golds for 1,500m, 5,000m, cross-country team & individual, 3,000-m steeplechase
1928 Olympics: 10,000m gold, 3,000-m steeplechase silver
23 world records at 11 different distances

He could have gone on to compete again in 1932, but he was banned because he broke the rules on amateurism that were in force at that time.

He achieved his Olympic successes at 1,500 meters, 3,000-meters steeplechase, 5,000 meters, and the cross-country race. No modern runner has ever won such a wide variety of titles.

Jesse Owens
U.S., 1913–80

Some athletes who participate in track and field events have been versatile enough to set records in a range of different events. One day in May 1935, Jesse Owens went one better than this. He became the only man ever to set a track and a field record on the same day, and the only man ever to set six world records in that one day, in fact gaining them all within one hour.

The 1936 Olympics were held in the German capital, Berlin. The Nazi dictator of Germany, Adolf Hitler, wanted to use the games to "prove" his racist theories, but instead the performance of Jesse Owens showed that such ideas were nonsense.

Owens won one team and three individual gold medals, two of them in world record times. Hitler was furious, but Jesse Owens came home in triumph.

▼ Jesse Owens winning one of his four 1936 gold medals. He took gold in the 100m, 200m, long jump, and, as part of the U.S. team, in the sprint relay.

Owens and Long
One of the reasons Hitler was so angry at Owens's win in the long jump was that the German athlete, Luz Long, was strongly favored for a medal. Although Hitler would have disapproved, Long helped Owens in the preliminary rounds of the event, so that Owens was able to get into the final.

Babe Zaharias
U.S., 1911–56

Babe Zaharias was a brilliant all-round sportswoman. She was an All-American basketball player in the early 1930s, and played in exhibition matches against the top male baseball players later in that decade. However, these sporting successes pale against her achievements in track and field.

In the 1932 Olympics, women were only allowed to enter three events. From her widely ranging choices, Babe won gold medals in the 80-meters hurdles and the javelin, and a silver in the high jump!

She was probably even better as a golfer. Her professional titles included the U.S. Women's Open in 1948, 1950, and 1954. She was one of the founders of the Ladies Professional Golf Association.

▼ Mrs Zaharias wins the 1947 British Women's golf championship, when she was still an amateur player.

▲ It's 1932 and no one can catch Mildred Didrikson.

Zaharias's original name was Mildred Didrikson. She earned her nickname, "Babe," in imitation of the great baseball player, "Babe" Ruth (see page 18). To complete her sporting connections, in later life she married an American professional wrestler, George Zaharias, and is now usually remembered by her married name.

Racket & Ball Wordsearch

Look for the words on the ball in the grid formed by the strings of the racket. Words may read up, down or diagonally. Some letters are used more than once, although never twice in the same word.

			T	A	N	S	W	E	R	S			
		S	I	H	S	U	K	N	O	C	K		
	E	M	E	X	I	C	O	S	W	I	N	G	
J	D	I	N	F	E	C	T	E	D	N	E	O	B
U	W	R	O	N	G	E	K	V	A	D	N	L	B
M	A	N	C	H	E	S	T	E	R	I	G	F	O
P	R	O	F	E	S	S	I	O	N	A	L	L	Y
S	D	V	E	L	E	C	T	I	O	N	A	E	S
	S	A	M	P	R	A	S	O	L	E	N	T	
		E	L	E	V	A	T	E	D	E	D		
			W	D	E	S	P	I	T	E			

MEXICO TEN
CREW SEVE
INDIAN NECK THICKEN
WRONG BOYS ANSWERS
HELPED SKEW ENGLAND
ELEVATED PROFESSIONALLY
ELECTION EDWARDS IDEAL
SMIRNOVA SAMPRAS SERVE
INFECTED DESPITE SOLE
KNOCK SUCCESS GOLF
JUMPS MANCHESTER
ARNOLD SIEGES
LET AIM

There are **34 WORDS** in the racket

Answers can be found on page 111

Index

Aaron, Hank 8, 15
Abdul-Jabbar, Kareem 20, 23
AC Milan 66, 73, 81
Ajax Amsterdam 66, 71, 81
"Albatross, The" 85
Alcindor, Al *see* Abdul-Jabbar, Kareem
All-American:
 basketball 21, 26, 27
 football 32, 33, 39, 40, 41
 tennis 87
Allen, Mark 96
Alpine Combined Events (skiing) 65, 64
Andrianov, Nikolai 51
Ashe, Arthur 87
Ashford, Evelyn 101
Atisanoe, Salevaa Fuali *see* Konishiki
Atlanta Braves 39
Atlanta Falcons 39
Australian Open (tennis) 87, 88, 93

Baggio, Roberto 67, 81
Ballesteros, Seve 42
Bannister, Roger 97
Barcelona 74, 76
Baseball Hall of Fame 9, 10
Basten, Marco van 81
Bayern Munich 68
Beckenbauer, Franz 68
Benfica 72
Best, George 69, 75
"Big Bird" 82
"Big Jack" 46
Bikila, Abebe 98
Bird, Larry 21
Blackpool 77
Blair, Bonnie 59
Blankers-Koen, Fanny 101
Borg, Björn 88, 89
Boston Celtics 21, 22
Boston Red Sox 13, 18, 19
British Amateur (golf) 44
British Open (golf) 42, 41, 44, 46, 47, 49, 50
Brooklyn Dodgers 16
Brown, Jim 32, 38

Bubka, Sergei 100
Burrell, Leroy 103
"Busby Babes" 75
Busby, Matt 75
Butkus, Dick 33

Canton Bulldogs 41
Caslavska, Vera 52
"Charlie Hustle" 17
Charlton, Bobby 70, 74, 75
Chicago Bears 33, 37
Chicago Bulls 22, 24
Cincinnati Reds 17, 39
Clemente, Roberto 9
Cleveland Browns 32
Cleveland Indians 19
Cleveland Spiders 19
Cobb, Ty 10, 17
Collegiate Woman Athlete of the Year 25
Comaneci, Nadia 53
Connors, Jimmy 87, 89
Copa Libertados 78
Cotton Bowl 35
Courier, Jim 95
Court, Margaret 90
cross-country 105
Cruyff, Johan 66, 71
Curtis Cup 50
Cuthbert, Betty 101
Cy Young Award 13

Dæhlie, Bjørn 62
Dallas Cowboys 39, 40
Davis Cup 87, 88, 93
Dean, Christopher 61
Detroit Red Wings 57
Detroit Tigers 10, 13
DiMaggio, Joe 11
Downing, Al 8
"Dream Team" 21, 23, 27
drugs in athletics 102, 103
"Dumptruck, The" 83

Eckert, Barbel 101
"Eddie the Eagle" 65
Edwards, Eddie 65
Els, Ernie 49
Emperor's Cup 82
Ender, Kornelia 84
European Cup 66, 69, 71, 72, 79, 81
European Cup Winners Cup 66, 71, 81
"European Pelé" 72
Eusébio 72
Evert, Chris 91, 96

FA Cup 75, 77
Federation Cup 94
Fighting Irish of Notre Dame 35
Finland 105
"Flo-Jo" 101
"Flying Finn" 105
Footballer of the Year: European 70
Footballer of the Year: FIFA 81
French Open (tennis) 88, 91

Gehrig, Lou 12
"Georgia Peach, The" 10
German Democratic Republic 84
Gibson, Bob 13
Giro d'Italia 29, 31
"Golden Bear" 46
Golden Glove awards 9
Graf, Steffi 91
"Grand Slam"
 golf 43 44, 45
 tennis 90, 91, 92, 93, 95
"Great One, The" 56
"Great White Shark" 47
Gretzky, Wayne 56, 57
Griffith-Joyner, Florence 101
Gross, Michael 85
gymnastics, men's 51

Harding, Tonya 59
Harlem Globetrotters 13
Hart Trophy 56
Hartford Whalers 57
Hawaii Ironman Championships 96
Heiden, Eric 59
Heisman Trophy 33
Herrera, Helenio 73
"His Airness" 24
Hogan, Ben 43
Honved 79
Houston Rockets 26
Howe, Gordie 56, 57

Indiana Pacers 25
Indurain, Miguel 29
Inter Milan 73

"Iron Horse" 12

Johnson, "Magic" 23
Johnson, Ben 103
"Joltin' Joe" 11
Jones, Bobby 43, 44
Jordan, Michael 22, 24, 26
Joyner, Al 101
Joyner-Kersee, Jackie 101
Juventus 67, 80

Kansas City Chiefs 35
Kerrigan, Nancy 59
King, Billie Jean 91, 92
"King of the Mountains" 31
Kintetsu Buffaloes 15
Kirishima 83
Koch, Marita 102
Konishiki 83
Korbut, Olga 53
Koss, Johann Olav 62

La Fleur, Guy 55
Landy, John 97
Latynina, Larissa 52, 54
Laver, Rod 93
Law, Denis 75
Leicester City 74
LeMond, Greg 30
Lewis, Carl 103
Lineker, Gary 74
Liverpool 75
Long, Luz 106
Longo, Jeanne 28
Lopez, Nancy 45
Los Angeles Dodgers 15
Los Angeles Lakers 20, 22, 23
LPGA Hall of Fame 50

maillot jaune 30, 31
Manchester United 69, 70, 75
Maradona, Diego 76
Marino, Dan 34
Martinez, Conchita 94
Matthaus, Lothar 81
Matthews, Stanley 77
Mays, Willie 14
McEnroe, John 88
Merckx, Eddy 31
Mets 14
Miami Dolphins 34
Miller, Cheryl 25
Miller, Reggie 25
Milwaukee Braves 8

Milwaukee Bucks 20
Montana, Joe 35, 38
Montreal Canadiens 55
Montreal Expos 17
Morceli, Noureddine 97, 104
Moser-Pröll, Annemarie 63
Most Valuable Player:
    baseball 9, 13, 14, 15, 17
    basketball 21, 24
    football 36, 37, 38, 40
Munich air disaster 70, 75

Naismith Award 25
Namath, Joe 36
Nancy 80
Napoli 76
Navratilova, Martina 91, 94
"Negro Leagues" 16
Negro National League 14
New Orleans Saints 37
New York Cosmos 68, 78
New York Giants 14, 34, 40
New York Jets 36
New York Yankees 11, 12, 18
Newby-Fraser, Paula 96
NFL's All-time Team 33
Nicklaus, Jack 46, 48
Nomo, Hideo 15
Norman, Greg 47

Nurmi, Paavo 105
Nykanen, Matti 65

O'Neal, Shaquille 27
Oh, Sadaharu 15
Olajuwon, Hakeem 26
Olazabal, Jose Maria 49
Orlando Magic 26, 27
Owens, Jesse 106
Ozeki 83

Palmer, Arnold 48
Payton, Walter 32, 37, 40
Pelé 78
Petrik, Larissa 52
Philadelphia Athletes 10
Philadephia Phillies 17
Pittsburgh Pirates 9
Pittsburgh Steelers 39
Platini, Michel 80
Player of the Year 50
Price, Nick 49
"Prime Time" 39
Puerto Rico 9
Puskas, Ferenc 79

Real Madrid 79
Rice, Jerry 35, 38
Richard, Maurice 55
Riggs, Bobbie 92
Robinson, Jackie 16
"Rocket" 55
Rodnina, Irena 60
Rose, Pete 17
Ross Trophy 56

Ruth, "Babe" 8, 12, 18
Ryder Cup 42

Samoa 83
Sampras, Pete 95
San Diego Chargers 38, 39
San Francisco 49ers 35, 38, 39
San Francisco Giants 14
Sanders, Deion 39
Santos 78
Sheehan, Patty 50
Smith, Emmit 40
Solheim Cup 50
Spitz, Mark 86
St Etienne 80
St Louis Cardinals 13, 19
Stanley Cup 55
steeplechase, 3,000-meters 105
Stefano, Alfredo di 79
Stoke City 77
Super Bowl 35, 37, 38, 39, 40
Szewinska, Irina 102

Taiho 82
Thorpe, Jim 41
Tomba, Alberto 64
Toronto Maple Leafs 55
Torvill, Jayne 61
"total football" 66
Tottenham Hotspur 74
Tour de France 28, 29, 30, 31

Triple Crown, baseball 12
Tumba, Sven 58

U.S. Amateur (golf) 44, 48
U.S. Masters (golf) 42, 41, 44, 46
U.S. Open: golf 43, 44, 45, 46, 48, 107
    tennis 87, 88, 89, 91, 92, 93, 95
U.S. Tour (golf) 49
U.S. Women's Open 50
UEFA Cup 66, 67, 73
Ulanov, Aleksei 60

Wanamaker Mile 104
Warner, Pop 41
Wimbledon 87, 88, 89, 91, 92, 93, 94, 95
World Club Championships (soccer) 73
World Cup: golf 58
    skiing 63, 64
    soccer 67, 68, 70, 71, 72, 74, 76, 78, 79, 80
    penalty shoot-outs 67
World Series 11, 13

Yokozuna 83
Yomiuri Giants 15
Young, Cy 19

Zaharias, Babe 107
Zaitsev, Aleksandr 60

Picture Acknowledgments

t = top; b = below

Allsport: 11t, 18b, 20t, cover & 20b, 22t, 26t, 26b, 28t, cover & 43t, 43b, 52, 69b, 70b, 75t, 80b, 85b, 89t, 89b, 90b, 91t, 91b, 92t, cover & 92b, 94t, 98b, 99t, 99b, 102t, 106b.
Allsport/Hulton Deutsch: 31t, 44t, 44b, 7 & 51, 54b, 69t, 70t, 71t, 71b, 72t, 72b, 77t, 77b, 82t, cover & 82b, 87t, 87b, 90t, cover & 97t, 97b, 98t, 106t, 107b.
Allsport/Inpho: 68t.
Allsport/MSI: cover & 68b.

Allsport/Agence Vandystadt: 28b.
Allsport/individuals: Bruno Bade 29t; Shaun Botterill 73t; Clive Brunskill 66t, 95t, 95b, 66b; Simon Bruty 74t, 81t, cover & 103t; David Cannon 50t, 45b, 46t, 47t, 47b, 48t, 48b, 49t, 49b, cover & 64t, 64b, 67t, 74b, 75b, 80t, 81b; Chris Cole cover, 76b; Glenn Cratty cover & 56t; J.D. Cuban 56b; Jonathan Daniel 22b, 24b, 35t; Tim Defrisco 27b, cover, 6 & 59t, 59b; Steve Dopaola 27t; Tony Duffy 25b, cover & 53t, 53b, 60b, 60t, cover, 1 & 61b, 61t, 85t, 86t, 88b, cover, 101b, 102b; Mike Dunn 23b; Stephen Dunn 23t;

John Gichigi 42t; Michael King cover & 85b; David Leah 76t; Bob Martin 62b, 94b; Don Morley 45t; Gary Mortimore 65t, cover & 100b, cover; Stephen Munday 42b; Gary Newkirk 96t, 96b; Mike Powell 29b, 100t; Steve Powell 46b, 88t, 103b; Ben Radford 73b; Pascal Rondeau 30t, cover, 7 & 65b; Rick Stewart 25t; Damian Strohmeyer 21t, 21b; Claudio Villa 67b; Anton Want cover & 55.
Archive: 10t, 17b.
Archive/ APA: 43t.
Archive/ Popperphoto: 93b, 105t.
Archive/ Reuters: 38b, 39, 40, 50t Shuan Best, 50b Koji Horimizu, 83t Ken

Igo, 83b, 104t Ray Stubbelbine, 104b Luciano Mellace.
The Bettman Archive: 10b.
Corbis-Bettman: 14t, 84t.
Corbis-Bettman/ Reuters: 30t, 30b, 38t, 39b.
Corbis-Bettmann/UPI: 8t, 8b, 9t, 9b, 11t, 12t, 12b, 13t, 13b, 14b, 16t, 16b, 17t, 18t, 19t, 19b, 32, 33t, 33b, 34t, 34b, 35b, 36t, 36b, 37t, 37b, 41t, 6 & 41b, 43b, 57, 84b, 86, 93t, 105b, 107t, cover Range.
Hulton Deutsch Collection: 54t, 84t.
Pica Pressfoto AB: 58t, 58b.
Popperfoto: 15t, cover & 15b, 63t, 63b, cover & 78t, 78b, 79t, 79b.